ART OF THE
SCRAPBOOK

ART OF THE
SCRAPBOOK

A GUIDE TO HANDBINDING AND DECORATING
MEMORY BOOKS, ALBUMS, AND ART JOURNALS

Diane Maurer-Mathison

WATSON-GUPTILL PUBLICATIONS / NEW YORK

Notes on the Art

On cover, clockwise from top left: Edge-sewn scrapbook by Doris Arndt; photo album with window cover decoration, by the author; book with stamped and thermal-embossed cover decoration by Lea Everse; scrapbook page collage, by the author; scrapbook with spiral-stitched binding by Gail Crosman Moore.
On page 2, top to bottom: Handmade papers with embedded flowers and ribbon-embellished cover decoration by Ruth Ann Petree; album pages by Ruth Ann Petree.
On pages 2–3 (background): Detail of hand-marbled silk by the author.

All line art provided by Jeffery Mathison.
All art not credited to a specific artist produced by the author.

Acknowledgments

Sincere thanks to all the book and paper artists who allowed me to show their innovative and inspiring works.

Senior Editor: Candace Raney
Editor: Julie Mazur
Designer: Areta Buk
Production Manager: Ellen Greene
Text set in 10.5-point Weiss

First published in 2000 by
Watson-Guptill Publications,
a division of BPI Communications, Inc.,
1515 Broadway, New York, NY 10036

Library of Congress Cataloging-in-Publication Data
Maurer-Mathison, Diane V., 1944–
    Art of the scrapbook : a guide to handbuilding and decorating memory
books, albums, and art journals / by Diane Maurer-Mathison.
        p. cm.
    ISBN 0-8230-1019-8
    1. Photograph albums.   2. Photographs—Conservation and restoration.
3. Scrapbooks.   I. Title.

TR465.M39 2000
745.593—dc21

                                                    99-089949

Printed in China

First printing, 2000

1 2 3 4 5 6 7 8 9 / 08 07 06 05 04 03 02 01 00

FOR JEFFERY AND JENNIFER

CONTENTS

PREFACE

An interest in making scrapbooks, photo albums, and art journals has been sweeping Europe and the United States for several years. Any trip to your local crafts, photography, or department store will provide you with an array of merchandise for making scrapbooks, "memory books," or albums to house your memorabilia. The Internet is full of "scrapbooking" discussion groups and bulletin boards, and magazines carry all sorts of articles about the trend. Most of these shops, magazine articles, and Web sites lead you to sources for die-cut shapes, cute stickers to decorate album pages, and wildly colorful background papers to place beneath your photos.

Some of those who were having great fun a few months ago are noticing with disappointment that there's a generic "gone overboard" look to the albums they're creating, and that some of their work is more garish than beautiful. These people, and many who recently joined the scrapbook movement, are looking for ways to go beyond the current craze—to learn simple papermaking, paper decorating, and bookbinding techniques that will allow them to create beautiful, unique books that really reflect their tastes and personalities.

This book is designed to show you how to make archival scrapbooks that can truly become family heirlooms, or wildly innovative art journals and albums in which you can recount your dreams and experiences, or just keep track of all the great sushi bars you've visited. The projects are varied, so beginners as well as experienced craftspeople can begin at the appropriate level to make albums for housing their memorabilia, art, favorite poems, photographs, and writings. Some of the softcover and accordion-fold albums are simple to make and can be created in less than an hour. Other more complicated edge-sewn bindings will take longer, but will be worth the effort and will teach fine craft techniques that can be used in many projects. The well-known paper artists and book artists who share their work and techniques in this book will inspire you to create your own innovative designs that will look anything but generic.

Opposite: Sherrill Kahn used sponge printing and embossing techniques to adorn the cover of this journal.

Right: These edge-sewn and stab-bound journals by Claudia Lee have handmade paper collaged covers with bead and stick bindings.

CHAPTER 1

HANDBINDING BASICS

If you've never made a book before, the thought of starting from scratch with some paper, board, glue, and thread—as the ancient bookbinders did hundreds of years ago—can be intimidating. There's a certain reverence afforded handbound albums, and most people feel a little in awe of the artisans who make them. Although some types of elaborate sewn bindings can be quite complex, the projects you'll encounter in this book are surprisingly easy. If you proceed step by step you'll soon be a handbinder, making your own beautiful paper and silk scrapbooks, albums, and art journals.

This chapter will introduce you to the some of the materials and equipment you'll be using, and will teach you the basic techniques of working with book board, paper, and cloth. You'll find advice on how to work with delicate, tissue-thin papers and silks as well as heavy, fibrous, handmade ones. It will introduce you to the best (and least expensive) kinds of book-making equipment and teach you how to use the tools and materials to create a work you'll be proud of. And finally, a section on conservation principles will ensure that any heritage albums or family scrapbooks you make will last for generations.

Handmade and machine-made papers in a variety of colors, textures, and weights can be used for book construction.

MATERIALS AND EQUIPMENT

Although the projects in this book vary in difficulty and the time required to produce them, most call for similar materials and equipment. (Extra supplies needed for specific projects are listed separately.)

Finding supplies should not be difficult. As an interest in bookbinding increases, more craft shops and art supply stores stock interesting papers, boards, and basic binding tools. If a local shop doesn't have what you need, consult the source directory at the back of this book for a mail-order art supply or bookbinding shop that will furnish you with a catalog and can ship materials and equipment to you within a few days.

MATERIALS

- *Paper.* Three general types of paper will be used in book construction: *cover paper, interior* or *text paper,* and *endpaper.* For each, the specific book you're making will determine a range of appropriate papers. If you're making a hardcover accordion-fold book, for example, your cover paper will need to be strong but thin and pliable, such as unryu rice paper, so that it can wrap around a piece of book board. If you're making a simple softcover album, you will need to use a more rigid piece of cover stock or thick handmade paper, which can stand alone as a cover. Your choice will also be influenced by how well the paper stands up to repeated handling without cracking or fraying, and whether it will accept glue without stretching horribly or disintegrating.

As for the interior, or text, pages, your choice will depend not only on the style of album you're making, but also on the types of artifacts, if any, you plan to show on its pages. If you intend your book to be used primarily as a journal, to be filled with words, drawings, stamped images, and an occasional flat ticket stub or pressed flower, the interior paper can be rather thin and still work fine. But if you intend to create a scrapbook that, for example, is a tribute to your seamstress grandmother and will contain some of the antique buttons and laces from her sewing basket, you'll need a much stronger paper that can withstand gluing and/or stitching. Note that no matter how heavy your interior pages are, they should still score and fold without cracking so you can use them in various ways.

Decorative papers can be used for endpapers, which line the insides of scrapbook covers, or as flyleaves, which go between the endpapers and the first and last text pages. Try using marbled or paste papers for these. Crinkled metallic papers or handmade papers with embedded flower petals can also add an exotic touch. Because these papers are used primarily as decoration rather than for any specific function, you can usually choose them by how well they complement your book's theme and the other materials being used.

You'll have no trouble finding attractive papers for any album application as there are literally hundreds of domestic, imported, machine-made, and handmade papers available at specialty paper and art supply stores. Offerings run the gamut from the subtly sophisticated to the brazenly outrageous, in myriad colors and textures, and made with bits of everything from petals to bark to bits of currency. A quick look in my flat file drawers reveals stores of decorative papers that include unryu, Thai crinkle paper, Indian bark paper, Thai reversible paper (which is laminated so each sheet is a different color on the reverse side), banana paper, Indian silk paper, velour and velvet papers, hemp papers, corrugated papers, papers with embossed designs, and handmade specialty papers made from flower petals, grass, pine needles, denim, and Alaskan husky fur, to name just a few. (Well, yes, I made that last one up, but someone's probably doing it by the time you read this!) Most handmade papers have a *deckle,* or untrimmed, edge that can add greatly to the beauty of the pages in your album. Paper houses often sell via mail order and can supply you with sample paper swatches to see, feel, and test for any potential problems.

You might also try visiting fine craft shows where professional papermakers and paper decorators show and sell their sheets. If you deal directly with the artist you can often avoid higher retail prices, and you may find one who will design custom sheets for your special projects. Making and decorating your own papers, of course, is also an option, and will be discussed in Chapter 5.

- *Other papers.* You will also need scrap paper, waxed paper, tracing paper, and sandpaper. Scrap paper will be placed under any paper or fabric being glued, and should be replaced immediately after use. (I like to use an old phone book and simply tear away pages with any inkling of glue on them.) Waxed paper will be placed over any areas that have been glued to prevent them from sticking to other parts of a project during pressing. Tracing paper will be placed over damp, glued paper being burnished to prevent it from being damaged during burnishing. And sandpaper will come in handy for smoothing the rough edges of book boards.

- *Fabric.* Several types of fabric can be used in book construction. The type most commonly used is *book cloth*, which is by far the best material for making a sturdy hinge for a hardcover book. Paper-backed book cloth is the easiest variety to use: It accepts glue well, doesn't stretch, and the paper backing prevents glue from seeping through and possibly staining the cloth. It's available from bookbinding suppliers and comes in many colors, patterns, and fabrics.

  Other fabrics, such as silk, rayon, cotton, and linen, can also be used in book construction. I often use hand-marbled silks to cover small accordion-fold photo albums; a favorite silk scarf can easily be recycled and made into an album cover this way. Padded covers can be made with pieces of antique quilts or tapestries and cotton batting. (For instructions on making fabric-covered books, see page 31.)

- *Book board. Book board*, also known as *binder's board* or *Davey board*, is used to create hard covers for books. Its thickness is measured with a point system, with 90-point board being one of the

Ruth Ann Petree uses handmade papers with embedded flower petals and ribbon-embellished cover decorations to give her books distinctive personalities.

heaviest and measuring approximately ¹/₁₆ inch (0.2 cm) thick. Thinner boards like mat board, museum board, photo mount, illustration board, and chipboard can also be used, depending upon the type of book you're making and whether you're using only archival materials. Art supply and bookbinding supply stores offer lots of choices. Although heavy boards require more patience to cut, they offer the benefit of being less likely to eventually warp. I don't recommend using foam core as it is easily dented.

- *Adhesives.* Paper and fabric are usually adhered to book board with glue or paste, although double-sided adhesive film is also sometimes used. I recommend using polyvinyl acetate (PVA) glues, like the many neutral pH adhesives available, as well as "Yes" Paste (all available in craft supply stores). PVA glues dry clear, are flexible, and can be thinned with water. "Yes" Paste, available at bookbinding and art supply stores, is a mixture of wheat starch and glycerin. One benefit of "Yes" Paste is that it won't wrinkle even the thinnest papers. It also dries quite quickly and can be thinned with water. (Always use distilled water to preserve an adhesive's archival properties.)

Other adhesives include methyl cellulose, wheat paste, and starch paste. As with all products, follow the instructions provided by the supplier for use. Glue sticks can be used successfully on small projects. Rubber cement should never be used as in just a few years it will bleed through papers and ruin them. (See page 20 for more information on working with adhesives.)

- *Removable tape.* Many projects require removable tape to temporarily secure elements while you work with them.
- *Bookbinding needles.* Needles should have eyes big enough to carry thread and thin cords.
- *Cords and ribbons.* Almost any strong, non-stretching ribbon or cord can be used to sew a binding or tie a book closed. Linen thread is usually preferred by professional binders, but decorative ribbons and cords can also be used to add character to edge-sewn bindings, and ribbons can be used to accent covers held together with other types of fasteners. Bookbinding supply houses, fabric shops, and jewelry supply catalogs offer lots of decorative braids and cords. You may also spot interesting possibilities in less traditional venues; one bookbinder friend discovered colorful binding cord at an awning company, and I once discovered spools of vintage rayon cord in subtle hues for one dollar each at a flea market. The cord was quite dingy on the outside, but only a half-inch into the spool it was pristine.
- *Other fasteners.* Posts, screws, and decorative rings can all be used to hold books together. Aluminum and brass posts are readily available through bookbinding supply and some office supply houses, and can be colored with paint pens appropriate for metal and plastic. Common screws, washers, and nuts can also be used to join covers and pages; try alternating types of metal or painting them to add interest. Jewelry supply catalogs offer giant 1-inch (2.5-cm) anodized aluminum jump rings in a dozen different colors, which are great for making ring-bound albums, as well as colorful aluminum wire that bends easily for creating spiral bindings.

Cords, ribbons, screw posts, sticks, wire, and decorative rings can all be used to bind your scrapbooks.

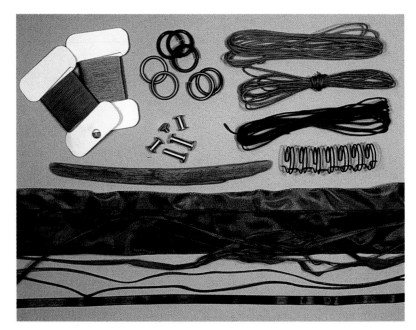

EQUIPMENT

For many of the items listed opposite, I've mentioned inexpensive substitutes that can be used in place of professional bookbinding equipment, so you can try your hand at the craft with minimal expense. Once you recognize that you've always been a closet bookbinder, however, you'd do well to invest in the best equipment you can afford. It will make your job easier and your books more beautiful.

- *Paper cutter.* A large paper cutter, preferably one with a bar to hold the paper in place, will allow you to cut several sheets at once and to easily divide sheets of paper and lightweight board for use in projects.

- *Craft knife and metal ruler.* If you don't have a paper cutter, you can make accurate cuts by using an X-acto knife and a metal straightedge or steel square to guide the blade. Heavy chipboard or Davey board should be cut with a mat or utility knife. Stock up on blades and always use a sharp one to make clean cuts.

- *Squaring devices.* A steel square will be indispensable for squaring and cutting book board, and a plastic triangle or smaller T-square will come in handy when folding papers for book interiors. One of my favorite tools is a plastic triangle with calibrations and grids for measuring and squaring, made by the C-Thru Ruler Company. The grid on this gem can be read on dark or light paper and the triangle has a metal edge for cutting, too.

- *Cutting mat.* A self-healing cutting mat should be placed underneath the paper or board being cut. Don't use cardboard for a cutting surface as it will rapidly dull your blades.

- *Scissors.* Different projects call for various types of scissors—some with long blades, some with short, decorative blades—to be used for constructing covers and creating decorative pages.

- *Clamps or clips.* These will be used to hold materials in place while you drill or punch spine holes through book covers and pages.

- *Hole punches.* Various types of paper punches and decorative hole punches can be used to make spine holes. A Japanese screw punch with different size bits is a great tool: When you apply pressure on the handle the bit rotates, creating a hole in paper or board. Look for them in bookbinding supply catalogs. Hardware supply hole punch sets can also be used for paper and board. You simply pound the punch with a rubber mallet to cut through the material to the cutting mat. Awls, drill presses, and hand-held drills (like those made by Fiskars) can also be used.

- *Awl or large weaving needle.* Awls are helpful for making holes in lightweight board and paper, and for scoring heavy papers to be folded.

- *Bone folder.* A bookbinder's bone folder is used for folding, scoring, and creasing papers. It is also used to press out air bubbles and wrinkles when gluing papers and fabrics to other surfaces.

- *Glue brushes.* Purchase a few large and small glue brushes, with the quantity of each depending on your project. Large brushes should be used to apply glue to large areas of book board, while small brushes are more convenient for coating small corner strips. Although many people love working with the traditional, large, round, natural-bristle bookbinding brushes, I find slightly stiff, flat, synthetic-bristle brushes from art supply stores fine for most jobs.

- *Damp sponge.* Always keep a damp sponge nearby when working with liquid adhesives. It will help remove any glue from your fingers before it gets transferred to your papers.

- *Book press.* Two smooth boards and a few heavy books or bricks can be used as a makeshift book press to prevent glued materials from warping as they dry. For small projects, heavy books alone will do the job. To make a paper press that can also be used for pressing books, see page 104.

Other materials and equipment used in specific projects or for paper decorating techniques will be noted in subsequent chapters.

Some of the equipment used in bookbinding.

If you intend to create books that will last for several generations, it is important to make sure that the materials you use and the environment in which the books are kept are conducive to longevity. A few hours spent in a frame shop witnessing the damaged art being brought in will convince any doubters that acidic materials like scotch tape, rubber cement, and picture mats made from wood pulp will deteriorate papers they come into contact with in only a few short years.

Luckily, most of today's paper manufacturers and producers of adhesives, paints, inks, and photo corners indicate which of their products are acid free (with a pH of 7 or more), which are both acid and lignin free (containing neither acid nor lignin, a component of wood pulp that can become acidic and cause acid-free paper to yellow and deteriorate within a few decades), and which are archival. The term *archival* usually refers to products that have a neutral pH and are neither acidic nor highly alkaline (which can also damage mementos). These products can be safely used in albums expected to last for generations. Papers are also available that are buffered with calcium carbonate, which will absorb any damaging acids that come into contact with the papers, although only for the life span of the buffer.

It makes sense to buy the best materials you can afford and to understand how to treat papers and photos so as to best preserve them. You can then decide which of your books you want to make sure will last for many generations and which, because they're designed only to bring pleasure during your lifetime, can be treated more

When creating an album intended to last for generations, it's important to use archival materials. These albums were created by Ruth Ann Petree.

casually. The following is a short primer on what to look for and what to avoid if you're concerned with making scrapbooks, albums, and art journals that will last as long as possible. Please note that companies selling archival supplies are listed in the source directory on page 143.

- *Paper and boards.* Avoid unbuffered papers and boards made from wood pulp, which contains acids that can turn paper brown and brittle nd actually eat holes through it. Acids can also migrate and turn acid-free papers and fabrics into acid-rich ones. A newspaper clipping or ticket stub made with really cheap paper placed on an acid-free backing will quickly contaminate both the page on which it rests and the one facing it when the album is closed. Use a color photocopier to copy anything on newsprint or other highly acidic paper onto acid-free paper. If you are in doubt as to a paper's acid content, check it with a pH testing pen, such as the inexpensive one made by Lineco. To use, simply draw a line on the material being tested. If the line turns lavender, it means that the material is acid free or neutral, with a pH of 6.8 or above. If the line turns yellow or remains colorless, the paper or board is acidic and should not be used.

    Some papers with low acidity will still discolor and begin to break down, but not for several decades. The most expensive papers— those made from cotton and linen or those that are calcium-buffered—are likely to last the longest. You might also consider adding buffered paper over acidic mementos to absorb some of their acid, replacing the paper as it ages. Other options include using neutral-pH glassine to isolate pages from each other or to make pockets for acidic materials (like flowers), spraying acidic papers with a de-acidifying product like Archival Mist (made by Preservation Technologies), or placing acidic documents or certificates in clear Mylar envelopes to prevent acid from escaping and ruining nearby items.

- *Photo sleeves.* If you like to use photo sleeves to house photos or other collections, make sure they are made of either polypropylene or polyethylene. Either of these plastics can contact photos without damaging them. Never use plastic photo sleeves containing polyvinyl chloride (PVC) as they release hydrochloric acid.
- *Adhesives.* Do not use cellophane tape, rubber cement, or glues with an acid or solvent content. There are many high-quality, acid-free glues available, as well as acid- and solvent-free double-faced adhesives, which come in sheets. Be sure that any adhesive photo corners you use are also acid free.
- *Inks and paints.* Only use permanent pens and inks that are labeled as archival. The ink from ballpoint pens often fades in a few short years and other inks can bleed onto or discolor papers they touch.

The environment in which you store your books is just as important as the materials you use to construct them. Photos, papers, and book cloth should be stored in the living area of your home, where the temperature is kept moderate all year round. Attics can overheat in the summer months and cause photos to become stiff and brittle. Heat also increases the rate of chemical reactions, which can lead to more rapid deterioration of your photos and other materials. Basements and garages, on the other hand, tend to be damp, and photos, papers, and other materials stored there will quickly become mildewed or acquire fungus growth. Such damage may not be obvious at first, but a sniff will often tell you that something nasty is going on. Paper-eating insects can also munch on your treasures in little-used spaces, and you won't notice their presence until it's too late.

    Books should be stored out of sunlight to protect them from heat and fading. And finally, avoid storing books in wooden drawers, near a wood-stove, or in rooms where smoking occurs, as you will risk putting acid back into your work.

If you haven't done bookbinding before, familiarize yourself with the following procedures before attempting them on expensive paper and boards. All are simple to do, but as with all new skills, you'll feel more comfortable after practicing them a few times.

FINDING A PAPER'S GRAIN

Book board and most machine-made papers, like planks of wood and pieces of fabric, have what's known as a "grain"—a direction in which the fibers align themselves. (This is as opposed to handmade papers, which are made of fibers distributed at random and usually do not have a particular grain direction.) In constructing scrapbooks, albums, and art journals it will be important to note and keep track of the grain direction of your materials and make sure they match. Papers with the fold line running *parallel* to the grain will crease easily without cracking, and will hold their shape. Papers folded *against* the grain will crease unevenly, will crack, and will generally uncooperative.

To test for grain direction in a sheet of paper, bend the sheet in half. If the paper easily collapses in on itself, you're bending with the grain. If the paper resists, you're bending across the grain. Test the paper in each direction and then pencil an arrow to mark the grain direction.

To test for grain direction in book board, hold the long edges of the whole sheet in your hands and attempt to bend it. Little resistance means the grain is running parallel to your arms; considerable resistance means you're bending across the grain. It's more difficult to run this test on smaller pieces of board, so always test uncut board first and then pencil arrows on each piece you cut to avoid losing track of the grain direction.

CUTTING

There are several ways to divide papers, boards, and book cloth. The easiest way to make straight cuts is with a good quality paper cutter. If you plan to make several books, it makes sense to invest in a good cutter with a bar that holds material in place while you lower the chopping arm.

TIP

Wet papers tend to curl with the grain, so when gluing them to book board it's important to make sure that the grain of both materials matches. If materials with opposing grain directions are glued together, they'll pull in opposite directions as they dry and will create a warped project.

You know you're bending *with* the grain if a sheet of paper collapses easily. If it offers resistance, you're bending *across* the grain.

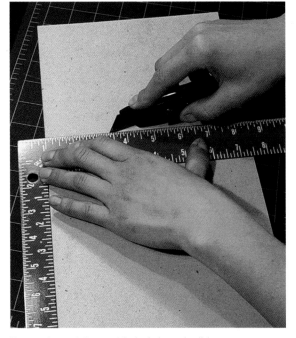

To cut through heavy binder's board, slide your mat knife along the edge of a metal ruler.

Care must be exercised in using this type of cutter as the blade will remain very sharp.

Most heavy mat board and book board is too thick to be cut on a moderately priced paper cutter, and can be divided more easily with a mat cutter (and a stock of sharp blades) or by using a mat knife with a fresh blade against the edge of a metal ruler. Work over a self-healing cutting mat and expect to make several cuts to divide your material cleanly.

Use an X-acto knife and metal ruler in the same way to slice through papers or paper-backed book cloth. Hold the knife upright and make sure you change blades often so cuts are clean, not ragged. Lightweight papers can also be cut with rotary paper trimmers, or with edging scissors for decorative cut edges.

TEARING

If you want your pages to have decorative edges that resemble the deckle edges of handmade paper, there are several ways to achieve them. A number of deckle-edge rulers on the market will loosely approximate the real thing if you hold the ruler in place over a sheet of paper and tear the paper against the edge of the ruler. (Design A Card makes one called the Art Deckle; see page 117.) You can also lay down a line of water with a wet brush, let the water soak into the paper, and then pull the paper apart. To create a free-form line, let the brush wander. To form a straighter edge, fold the paper or run the wet brush against a ruler. Highly fibrous paper will be more easily torn if you keep the tear line parallel to the grain of the paper. You can also divide paper by tearing it without the water assist. Tear the paper toward you to expose part of the paper's core, or away from you to create a clear but ragged edge.

SCORING AND FOLDING

Scoring—using a bone folder, awl, weaving needle, or other tool to crease a paper's surface— prepares a paper for folding and creates sharper, neater fold lines. Folding with the grain of the paper is recommended, although some papers, no matter what you do, will remain uncooperative

Thick or highly fibrous papers will be easier to tear if you wet the paper first, then tear parallel to the paper's grain.

and resist folding crisply. It's best to test a paper to see how well it folds before investing in a large number of sheets.

To score, hold a plastic or metal triangle or other squaring device against the desired fold line. Using the triangle to guide you, drag the point of the scoring tool down the length of the triangle. Your goal is to indent—not to break—the surface of the paper to prepare it for folding. Then bend the paper *away from* (rather than *into*) the fold line to crease the sheet.

WORKING WITH ADHESIVES

The decision of whether to use archival glue, paste, a glue stick, or adhesive film to bond papers and fabrics will depend upon the kind of project you're working on and its intended life span. While spray adhesives and adhesive films, like Cello-Mount (made by Cello-Tak), will make your work go faster, some may produce a weaker bond, so read labels carefully. When using liquid glue, work as quickly as possible to avoid having one area of the paper or board dry while you're working on another.

Always work over a sheet of scrap paper (with lots more at hand) and work from the center toward the edges, spreading glue evenly over the entire surface of the paper or board. Although

some book artists like to apply glue over an entire sheet of paper or fabric and then lay the book board on the glued sheet, I find it much easier and neater to apply glue to the book board and then apply the glued board to the paper or fabric, brushing on more glue when it's time to adhere the paper or fabric over the edges of the board. Most projects in this book will call for using this second technique, although you should use whichever you prefer. I've found applying glue to the board lessens problems with paper wrinkling—especially for novice bookbinders. (It also lessens the likelihood of transferring glue to your fingers and visible parts of your book.)

There are also a number of double-sided adhesive films on the market that can be used. Some, like Cello-Mount, consist of a thin sheet of adhesive film sandwiched between two slippery protective papers. To use the film, you peel away one protective sheet to expose the adhesive, then apply your board, paper, or book cloth to it. When you peel away the other protective sheet, you're left with a sticky-backed piece of book board, paper, or book cloth.

Other mounting adhesives, like those made by Specialty Tapes or Neschen, consist of a roll of very thin adhesive coated onto release paper. Because it's not double sided, this type of adhesive

To score a sheet of paper, drag the point of your scoring tool down the length of a metal or plastic triangle. Then bend the paper away from the fold line to crease the sheet.

is a bit trickier to use, but its adhesive properties are great and some, like the Gudy-870 Mounting Adhesive from Neschen, are acid and solvent free.

All of these products come with tips for using them and the suggestion that you practice before using them on a project. When you're working with liquid glue, there's a window of opportunity during which you can shift your book board or other material into position if you miss the mark. But if your book board is backed with a dry mounting adhesive, you get only one shot, so it's a good idea to practice first.

BURNISHING

Burnishing is an important step in creating good bonds between glued book boards and the papers that cover them. After your board has made contact with the paper or fabric that will cover it, turn the board over so the paper or fabric faces up. Working from the center outward, use the side of a bone folder to push out any wrinkles or air bubbles. Avoid adding a shine to the paper or fabric by working over a piece of tracing paper or other lightweight paper. You should burnish bonds made with double-sided adhesive film, too, as air bubbles can weaken them.

Burnishing will also help you fold scored papers, making sharp creases that can give a neater appearance to folds and help accordion-folded books open, close, and stand correctly. To avoid adding a shine to papers being burnished, you may want to work over a piece of tracing paper here, too.

PRESSING

Papers and fabrics that have become wet with glue tend to stretch at first and then shrink back as they dry, a process that can cause the book boards they cover to warp. To prevent warping, be sure to use pressure when drying any projects made with wet adhesives. A professional book press is ideal for this, but a couple of flat, smooth pressing boards with heavy books or bricks on top will also do the trick. (If you have already built a press for making handmade papers, as described on page 104, you can also use it for books.) Before you press, be sure to interleave wet areas with waxed paper to prevent glue from seeping out. Then leave the project under pressure overnight to dry thoroughly.

DRILLING OR PUNCHING

Various hole-punching devices can be used to create openings for binding your books with rings, screws, laces, and other types of fasteners. The type of fastener and the thickness of your book will determine the best tool to use. For example, if you're binding your book with screw posts, which completely cover the holes made, you can use a drill press and power drill without worrying about how cleanly the holes are cut. If you're creating an edge-sewn book with thin decorative cord, however, the edges of the holes will show and you will probably want to use a handheld punch to make holes with smoother edges. When working with punches, keep the punch upright so holes are not made at an angle, and clean the punch often by using a pin or the point of an X-acto knife to remove accumulated paper. When working with a hand drill, remember to rotate the handle counterclockwise after drilling to back out of the hole cleanly and avoid tearing the paper.

You will also need clips or clamps to keep pages and covers from moving when making holes, and a self-healing mat (or board, if drilling) to protect your work surface. In addition, you'll want to make a hole guide out of heavy paper or lightweight book board (see illustration, page 46). This will help you quickly line up and mark spots where holes should be made when repeatedly punching stacks of paper or creating similar books.

When burnishing papers to help bond them to boards, work from the center outward to push out any wrinkles or air bubbles.

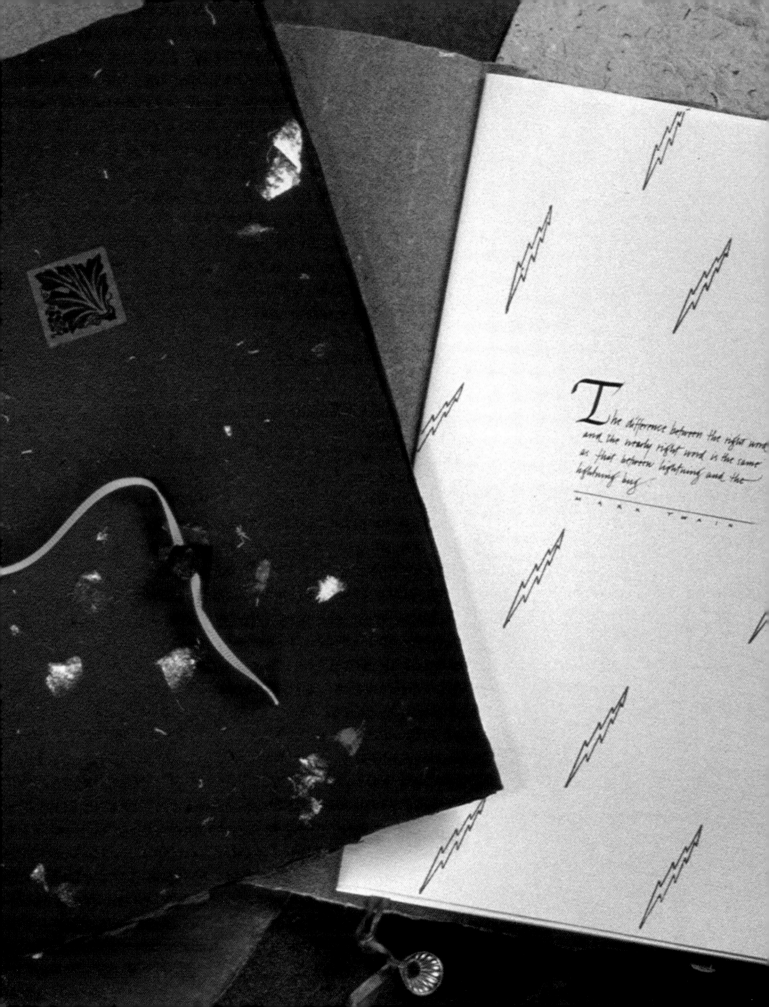

The difference between the right word and the nearly right word is the same as that between lightning and the lightning bug.

MARK TWAIN

CHAPTER 2

SIMPLE BINDINGS

Although you'll no doubt eventually want to create large and elaborate albums to house antique family photographs, button collections, or other treasures, it's worthwhile to start with some less complicated designs. The simple projects in this chapter can be made in an afternoon and will help prepare you for some of the more complex (and even more fun) bindings in Chapter 3.

Pamphlet-stiched books with
attached ribbons and beads, by
Ruth Ann Petree.

BASIC TIED BINDING

This most basic type of binding can be made in only a few minutes and is best used for books with soft covers. Here it is employed to bind a very simple book that can serve as a day journal for sketches and thoughts or to mark a special event.

WHAT YOU'LL NEED

- Light- to medium-weight text paper for text block
- Heavy handmade paper or decorated watercolor paper for soft covers
- Cord, raffia, or other material to tie book closed

BASIC TECHNIQUE

Decide what size book you want to make, then measure and cut a text block (the set of interior pages). If you want your book to hold some photos or flat memorabilia, try working with a heavier cover-weight paper like Canson Mi-Teintes and placing *spacers* between the pages of the book to thicken its spine. Spacers are strips of the same paper used for the text block, each about 1 inch (2.5 cm) wide and as tall as your text block. When attached to the spine edge of each page, they create filler space, so that when photos, wine labels, or other paper ephemera are inserted, pages will still lie flat instead of expanding upward. Use a glue stick to attach one spacer to each page so they'll stay in place later when you drill or punch your holes. (For an alternate way to add spacers, see tip on page 45.)

Cut two heavy papers the same size as your text block, or slightly larger, for the covers. (Note: If working with a flexible paper, you can cut one long piece of paper to use as both a front and back cover. Wrap it around the text block before punching holes.) If you're using heavy watercolor paper, the front cover will open more easily if you create a sort of hinge by scoring it vertically on the right (good) side. To do this, run a bone folder against a metal rule down the cover's spine edge, about 1 inch (2.5 cm) in from the spine.

Clamp or clip the covers and text block as shown opposite, keeping them flush along the spine edge. Drill or punch two holes about 3/4 inch (1.9 cm) in from the spine and 1 inch (2.5 cm) in from the book's top and bottom edges (its *head* and *tail*). Pass each end of your cord or other material through one of the holes from the back and tie the book closed, as shown opposite.

TIP

If bookmaking is new to you, it may help to familiarize yourself with the parts of a book before beginning the projects that follow.

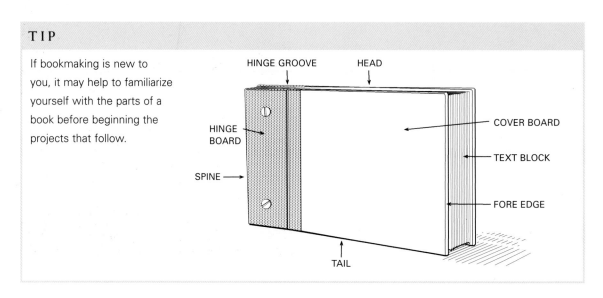

HINGE GROOVE   HEAD

HINGE BOARD

COVER BOARD

TEXT BLOCK

SPINE

FORE EDGE

TAIL

Using a Japanese hole punch to create a hole in the clamped journal.

The finished book, with a basic tied binding and handmade paper cover.

VARIATION: RUBBER-BAND-AND-STICK BINDING

Instead of ribbon or cord, this version of the simple binding is assembled by using a chopstick, piece of metal tubing, or other rigid device and holding it in place with a rubber band.

Begin by making a basic tied binding as just described. After punching the two holes, pass the ends of a long, strong rubber band through the holes from back to front. (Bend a paper clip to fish the ends of the rubber band through if necessary.) Hold the rubber band in place by slipping a strong stick or similar device through each end, with the remainder of the rubber band spanning the back of the book. Try using an object that coordinates with your book's theme, such as a shish kebab skewer or fork handle for a recipe album, or a long pencil for a collection of grade-school report cards. Decorative elastic braid can be substituted for the rubber band if tied or stitched securely.

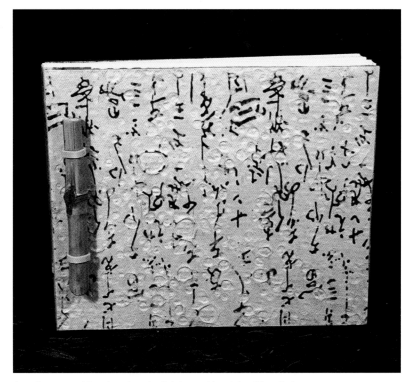

A softcover rubber-band-and-stick-bound book by Claudia Lee.

PAMPHLET-STITCHED BINDING

Like the basic tied binding, the pamphlet-stitched binding can be done with little effort and is best used for softcover books, like the one described below.

WHAT YOU'LL NEED

- Light- to medium-weight text paper for text block
- Heavy handmade paper or decorated watercolor paper for soft covers
- Cord, raffia, or other material to tie book closed

BASIC TECHNIQUE

Decide what size book you want to make, then double the width of one page to measure and cut spreads, rather than individual pages, for the text block. Fold each spread in half to form pages, burnishing the crease flat. If the grain runs vertically, the paper will be easier to fold. Make the cover by cutting a piece of cover-weight paper ¼ inch (0.6 cm) taller and ½ inch (1.3 cm) wider than an unfolded text page. A thick handmade sheet is a good choice. Fold this in half, too.

Gather the creased pages, center them inside the creased cover, and open the book so the cover is facing you. Now clamp everything together (with the book still open) and make three equidistant holes in the fold line or gutter of the book, passing through the cover and text block. I generally make mine 1 inch (2.5 cm) in from the head and tail of the book, with the third hole centered between them, but placement can vary as per your own design preference.

Cut a length of cord or other stitching material 2½ times the height of the cover. Pass the cord through the center hole in the cover, as shown in the diagram below, leaving a tail 8 inches (20 cm) or longer extending on the outside. Now carry the cord up the inside spine of the book and enter the top hole (A), bringing the cord back out toward you. Carry the cord down the outside spine of the book (bypassing the center hole) and down through the bottom hole (C). Pull the cord taut as you continue. Carry the cord up the inside spine again and through the center hole (B). Position the two ends of the cord (the original tail and the new end you just brought through) so that they straddle the length of cord already running down the outside spine, and tie them together to finish. If you prefer, you can begin sewing on the *inside* of the folded pages and knot the tails together inside to finish the book.

Ruth Ann Petree often adds whimsical elements to the covers of her books. Some of her pamphlet-stitched bindings are shown below, along with a matching card and trinket box.

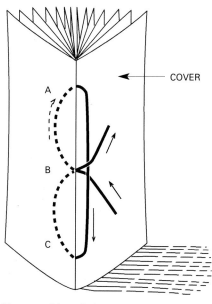

The pamphlet stitch.

COVER

RING BINDING

Decorative rings are an easy way to bind either hard- or softcover books, making them a favorite for artists who want to embellish pages and covers, not spend hours creating them. Here, rings are used to bind a casual hardcover album that can hold plenty of paper ephemera.

WHAT YOU'LL NEED

- Cover-weight paper for text block
- Book board for hard covers
- Decorative text-weight papers to wrap covers
- Text-weight paper for endpapers (to line the insides of the covers)
- Decorative rings (available in hardware or jewelry supply stores)

BASIC TECHNIQUE

Because they are a bit more complex, the instructions for this project have been separated into three stages: preparing the covers, creating the endpapers, and preparing the text block and binding the book. To make a softcover ring-bound book, follow the directions for a basic tied binding (page 24) but do not score the cover. Then use rings instead of ribbon to secure the covers and pages.

PREPARING THE COVERS

Decide what size you'd like your book to be and transfer the measurements to a piece of book board, making sure that the grain of your board runs vertically. Use a mat knife and T-square to cut out front and back cover boards. Check to be sure that the corners are cut at right angles and

A hardcover ring-bound album, like the one shown below, is simple to make and can expand to hold lots of material.

that all edges are straight. If the cutting leaves any ragged edges, lightly sand them.

Check the grain direction of the decorative paper you've chosen to cover the boards and arrange the paper on your worktable so the grain matches that of your cover boards. Cut two pieces, each 1 1/2 inches (3.8 cm) wider and longer than the book covers to allow a 3/4-inch (1.9-cm) border around each board. Place each board in the center of the back of the decorative paper you just cut and lightly trace positioning marks to help you gauge where to place the board when

Brushing a thin layer of glue onto a cover board.

Cutting the corners of the decorative cover paper.

you glue it down. (After you gain experience you can omit this last step, but beginners usually find it helpful.)

Prepare to glue the front board by placing it on a sheet of scrap paper. Working from the center outward, brush on a thin layer of glue. Place the board glue-side down within the positioning marks on your decorative sheet. Immediately discard the scrap paper and wipe any glue from your hands before turning the decorative paper and attached book board right-side up. Place a piece of tracing paper over the decorative paper and, using a bone folder, burnish from the center outward to remove any air bubbles or wrinkles.

Flip the board and paper over onto a clean piece of scrap paper so that the back of the book board is again facing up. Cut off the corners of the decorative paper, leaving about 1/8 to 1/4 inch (0.3 to 0.6 cm) between each corner of the board and the edge of the paper. Generally, twice the thickness of the book board is a sufficient margin of paper for covering the board's corners. Apply glue to one long edge of paper, running the brush against the lip of the book board as you work. Then fold the flap of paper over the book board to glue it down. (I like to stand the book on its edge for a moment and then lower it until it is flat to press the flap of paper down. If you have difficulty positioning the glued flaps, you may find that prefolding them before applying glue makes the job easier.) Use your thumb and then the bone folder to smooth the edge of the cover paper against the side of the book board, then burnish the paper down to remove any wrinkles or loose edges. Follow the same procedure for the other long flap, gluing it down and then burnishing it smooth.

To create neat corners, use your index fingernail or the tip of the bone folder to tuck in the small overlap of paper that appears when the long flaps are folded over (shown in the close-up diagram opposite). This overlap will prevent the corners of the board from showing when the shorter flaps of paper are folded over. Once the overlaps are tucked into place (angled slightly toward each other, as shown) apply glue to the remaining short paper flaps, fold them over, and burnish them in place. Repeat the entire process to cover the second book board for the back cover.

Applying glue to one long paper edge before folding it over the book board.

When working with small books, stand the book on its edge after applying glue to the paper flap. Then simply roll it over, apply pressure for a moment, and rub the edge in place with your thumb.

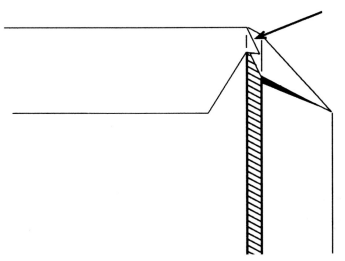

Be sure to tuck in the little overlap of paper (indicated with an arrow) to form a tight corner.

TIP

The process of cutting, folding, and fitting paper over the corners of the boards they cover is called *mitering*. Well-mitered corners are the mark of a good craftsperson. It pays to practice this operation a few times as a poor mitering job can ruin an otherwise attractive book.

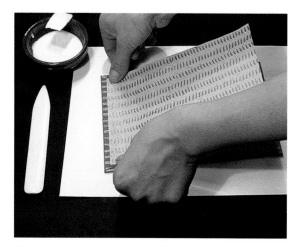

Gluing an endpaper to the inside of a book cover.

Working from the center outward to burnish the glued endpaper in place.

A finished ring-bound album. Layered papers form a background for the faux tile cover decoration, which Lynell Harlow created using dry embossing, stenciling, and rubber stamp embossing techniques.

CREATING THE ENDPAPERS

The papers used to line the insides of book covers are called *endpapers*. To make your endpapers, cut two pieces of text-weight paper $1/2$ inch (1.3 cm) shorter and narrower than the cover boards. This will allow for a $1/4$-inch (0.6-cm) margin of board on all four sides. Make sure that the grain of the endpapers runs vertically, matching that of the covers.

Apply glue to the back of one endpaper and align its edge about $1/4$ inch (0.6 cm) in from the left-hand side of your exposed front cover board. If you like, you can pencil a line or make a tiny prick with an awl to help you position the paper. When the endpaper is in position, use your fingers to rub it smoothly down, pressing out any air bubbles as you work. Once it is completely down, cover it with tracing paper and use a bone folder to burnish it down, working from the center outward to make sure it adheres well. Repeat the same process to glue the second endpaper onto the back cover board, then wrap both covers in waxed paper and press until dry.

PREPARING THE TEXT BLOCK AND BINDING THE BOOK

Cut or tear pages for the book. Pages should be about $1/2$ inch (1.3 cm) shorter and $1/4$ inch (0.6 cm) narrower than the book covers to allow for a $1/4$-inch (0.6-cm) margin around the head, tail, and fore edge. When the covers are dry, use a pencil to mark where you want the holes to be and center the pages vertically inside the covers, with the spine edges flush.

Clamp the stack of paper and board, using a piece of mat board or folded paper below the clamp to avoid damaging the covers. If you are using a drill press or hand drill, create the ring holes. If you're using a punch, make a heavy paper template to note where the holes should be placed as you'll need to punch several times to get through the stack of paper (see illustration, page 46). When the holes are completed, open the rings, pass them thorough the layers of paper and board, then squeeze them back together to finish binding the album.

Paper isn't the only material that can be used to wrap the boards of a hardcover book—fabric also makes a lovely covering. To use fabric, you'll need book boards, silk or another lightweight fabric, and double-sided adhesive film.

First, determine the size book you want to make and cut two cover boards. Iron your fabric, then stretch a piece large enough to cover the fronts of both boards side by side, with a 3/4-inch (1.9-cm) turnaround surrounding each board. (This means that you will need 1 1/2 inches [3.8 cm] of fabric between the two boards so that each will have a 3/4-inch [1.9-cm] turnaround on the shared side.) Pin the fabric to a piece of foam core or similar material to secure. Now cut a piece of paper-covered adhesive film just a hair smaller than the stretched fabric, peel off the backing paper, and smooth the adhesive paper onto the silk, burnishing it down.

With the silk still stretched, peel off the second layer of release paper and place the book boards onto the adhesive-backed silk as shown below. Using an X-acto knife, cut the fabric down the middle between the two boards, leaving a 3/4-inch (1.9-cm) margin of fabric on each side of your cut. Use the same knife to cut the edges of the silk away from the pins, but don't cut the corners of the silk off at an angle to miter them. It's easier to miter the corners by simply folding the silk over at each corner, as shown.

Fold over the longer flaps of adhesive-backed silk, pulling them toward the centers of the book boards with your fingers so they're snug. Finish both covers by folding over the short ends of the silk. Turn the cover boards over and burnish the silk (using tracing paper) to make sure all parts of it are well adhered.

Front and back cover boards placed on the stretched and adhesive-covered silk.

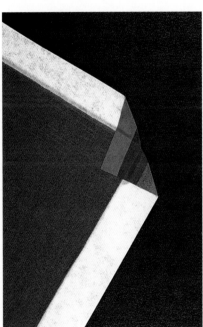

When working with thin fabric, it's easiest to miter the corners by simply folding the material over the corners of the book board.

A silk-covered accordion-fold book. I marbled this silk especially for the project, but you can purchase fabric or recycle a scarf to make a similar book. (See page 32 for instructions on making an accordion-fold book.)

ACCORDION-FOLD BINDING

A design of Eastern origin, the accordion-fold or concertina book is essentially one long piece of folded paper enclosed between two hard covers. It's a very versatile type of book, capable of holding photos or memorabilia on both the front and back of each folded page. Here, the basic binding is used to make a simple scrapbook. If made with heavy cover stock and with pages nearly as tall as the covers, this book can stand open for display. Make the book in any size, with or without ribbon ties or other type of closure.

WHAT YOU'LL NEED

- Cover-weight paper for folded text block
- Book board for hard covers
- Light- to medium-weight decorative paper to wrap covers
- Ribbon or cord to tie book closed (optional)

BASIC TECHNIQUE

The three basic stages of making an accordion-fold binding include preparing the covers, creating the text block, and assembling the book.

PREPARING THE COVERS
Follow the directions on pages 27–28 for the ring-bound album, but stop before making the endpapers. Sandwich the finished covers between pieces of waxed paper to keep glue from reaching other surfaces, and press them while you continue with the instructions below.

CREATING THE TEXT BLOCK
To determine the height of your text pages, measure the height of your cover and subtract 1/4 inch (0.6 cm). This will provide a 1/8-inch (0.3-cm) margin above and below the endpapers when they're glued to the book covers. (The margin must remain narrow if you want the book to stand open to display its contents.) To determine the

A hardcover accordion-fold book closed with ribbon ties. This book makes a great expanding photo album. If heavy paper is used for the pages, it can stand open for display.

width of the pages, measure the width of the cover and subtract ¼ inch (0.6 cm).

Use a large paper cutter or a mat knife and ruler to cut a long strip of cover-weight paper. The strip should be as wide as the *height* of your text pages, with the grain running across the width of the strip. (Don't worry about the length of the strip; you can cut several strips and join them later if necessary.)

Prepare to fold the pages by measuring each page width down the entire length of the paper strip, lightly marking each off with the tip of an awl or a needle. Place your squaring triangle at *every other* mark and score the paper by lightly running an awl or weaving needle against the edge of the squaring device. Then turn the paper over and score the remaining pages on the opposite side.

Create the first page by folding along the first score, folding *away* from the indentation, and then use your bone folder to crease the fold. For the next score, fold *toward* you, then continue down the strip, folding back and forth until you reach the end, making sure the top and bottom edges of the paper always line up. To add pages to your book, join similarly folded pages together using either of the two methods illustrated below.

TIP

A renegade method of folding—which goes much faster than the one just described—involves measuring and scoring for only the first fold, then turning the paper over and using the first folded page as a guide for scoring and folding the next. As you keep turning your paper over, make sure the tops and bottoms of your pages line up. If you always use the *previous* fold as a guide, you may find, as I do, that it works perfectly and that page size remains constant. Although this method is frowned upon by many and deemed impossible by some, it's worth a try. You, too, may be a gifted folder!

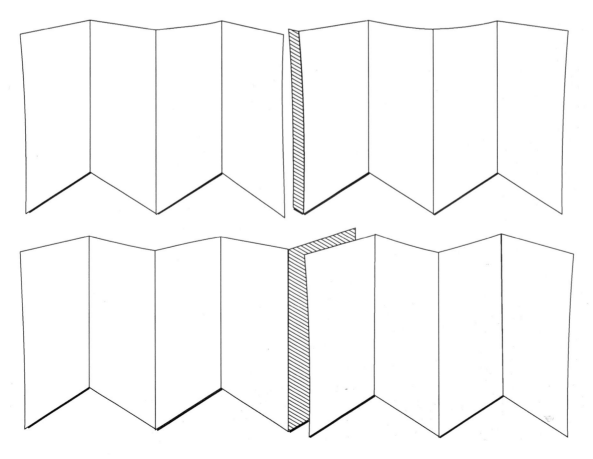

To create a longer accordion-fold book, overlap and glue folded strips together, using either method shown here.

ACCORDION-FOLD BINDING

Paper sculptor Nancy Cook created this accordion-fold book for her granddaughter, to commemorate the day they spent watching butterflies in Nancy's garden.

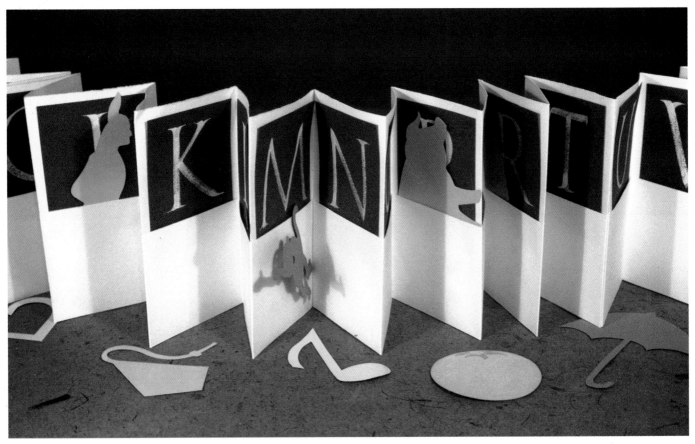

The accordion-fold design is amazingly versatile. An alternate version, which involves scoring and folding a horizontal section of the pleated pages *up* to form a pocket, is shown here in the work of calligrapher Gail Brown. A first scrapbook/alphabet book for a grandchild, each pocket holds a silhouette of an object or animal relating to the letter shown. Gail plans to add text (comments by the child) as the child grows.

Finish your strip by cutting off any excess that's too narrow to be used as a page, or that folds in the wrong direction. (The first and last pages of your book will be used as endpapers and should both fold toward the center of the book if you want the covers to face each other when the book is closed. Alternatively, they can be made to fold opposite each other.)

ASSEMBLING THE BOOK

If you wish to add ribbon ties to your book, apply a thin line of glue horizontally across the inside of the back cover and press ribbon (or another material) onto the glue. The left side of the ribbon should be long enough to extend around the back of the folded pages and over the front cover to tie with the end that extends from the right.

Once the ribbon has dried (if you have chosen to use ribbon), brush glue on the first and last pages of your folded stack and position them as endpapers within the book covers so that a ⅛-inch (0.3-cm) margin surrounds them. Use your bone folder over a sheet of tracing paper to burnish the endpapers down. Insert sheets of waxed paper between the endpapers and the new first and last pages of the book to keep any excess glue from penetrating, then press the book until dry.

VARIATION: ACCORDION-SPINE BINDING

The accordion-spine binding is comprised of a series of narrow accordion folds that extend from a center fold in a sheet of heavy cover stock. By using adhesive film or glue to attach heavy paper to one side of each pleat, you can make a very simple expanding album, as shown at right. Alternatively, holes can be punched in a pleated spine and then additional pages sewn on with a pamphlet stitch (see page 26). Book board covers can then be added as in the previous projects, or the first and last pages of the text block can simply be left as soft covers. In yet another variation, envelopes can be sewn into the valleys of the accordion folds to create an album with pockets for holding memorabilia. (See Deborah Waimon's book, shown on page 36.) As in Deborah's book, the envelopes are hand-folded and glued together after the stitching is done.

Positioning the glued endpaper in place on the front cover. Note the back cover with ribbon glued in place, waiting nearby to be attached to the back endpaper.

Accordion-fold books with rubber stamping and ribbon ties by Ruth Ann Petree.

A simple expanding album with an accordion-fold spine can be made by making narrow pleats in the center of a piece of heavy cover stock and then gluing heavy paper onto one side of each pleat.

ACCORDION-FOLD BINDING

Deborah Waimon used edging scissors and hole punches to create decorative cut pages for her accordion-spine binding.

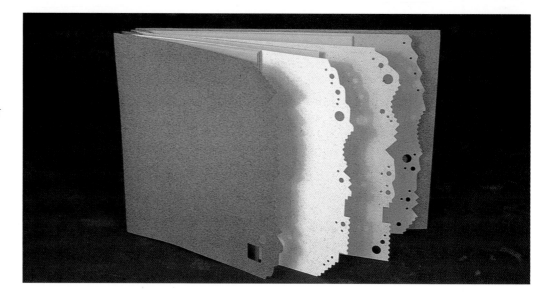

Raymond Rooster III, an accordion-spine storybook photo album by Judy Jacobs. Judy's variation of the basic accordion-fold structure includes fabric-covered cover boards, decorative stitching, and a band that restricts expansion of the album. PHOTO BY BILL WICKETT

Another variation of the accordion-spine book. This one by Deborah Waimon includes envelopes for holding memorabilia.

LAGUNA BINDING

This binding for a hardcover photo album or scrapbook was sent to me by John Balkwill, a book artist from the Lumino Press, in California. Although the directions are extensive, the binding is not difficult to make and uses many techniques covered earlier in this chapter.

As John explains:

The Laguna album is based upon the concept of adhering a series of simple folios (single sheets of paper, folded once) back to back at the spine and fore edge to create a series of double-thick pages onto which photographs can be mounted. When done properly, the album will open with good flexibility, lie flat when open, and be surprisingly sturdy.

Note that pages are formed by joining adjacent leaves of folded sheets, not by attaching a folded sheet to itself. The resulting design leaves two free endpapers that will eventually be glued in place to line the front and back covers.

The directions that follow, which are based on those John provided but have been slightly modified, are for a 10- × 8-inch (25- × 20-cm) horizontal hardcover album with fifteen page openings, plus endpapers. You can alter the directions to make smaller or larger albums as desired.

BASIC TECHNIQUE

The directions for this binding have been divided into three stages: creating the text block, preparing the covers, and assembling the book. Notice that for this project, the text block is created *before* the covers, instead of vice-versa as in previous projects.

CREATING THE TEXT BLOCK

Start by folding the sheets of heavyweight paper and endpapers in half, then trim each folded sheet to the desired size for your text block. (The folios are more likely to be cut correctly if they are trimmed to size *after* folding.)

The ³/₄-inch-wide (2-cm-wide) paper strips will be used as spacers to thicken the spine edge of the text block so that the book will lie flat when photos are added. Cut the strips to the same height as your text block, then apply one spacer to the outside of each *folded* edge, as shown on page 38. Use adhesive film to attach the spacers, or apply glue and press each sheet to its attached spacer to prevent wrinkling.

Once the spacers are attached, retrieve one of the folded and trimmed endpaper sheets and, leaving one half of the sheet free, apply glue to

A Laguna binding by John Balkwill of the Lumino Press (with cover papers by the author).

WHAT YOU'LL NEED

- Fifteen sheets of heavyweight 8¹/₂- × 20¹/₂-inch (22- × 52-cm) paper, such as Arches BFK 250gsm, for text block. The paper's grain should run in the 8¹/₂-inch direction.
- Fifteen ³/₄-inch-wide (2-cm-wide) paper strips, cut from the same heavyweight paper as the text block, for spacers
- Two sheets of similar (though perhaps darker) paper for endpapers
- Book board for spine and hard covers
- Decorative paper to wrap covers
- Book cloth for spine

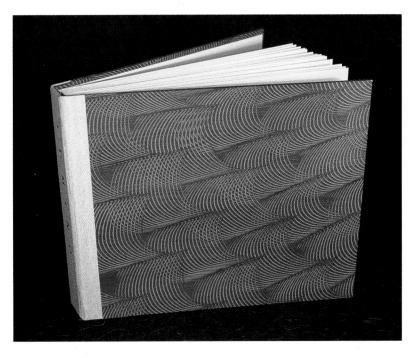

the fore edge and near the fold of the other half, as shown below. (To avoid getting glue on the rest of the page, John suggests you mask off part of the page with scrap paper and leave only a $^3/_4$-inch-wide [1.9-cm-wide] strip exposed on each side to receive the glue.) Working quickly, jog the pasted-up page to one of your folded folios. When the edges are matched up, burnish the pasted areas to secure the two folded sheets together. Place under a weight to dry. (Adhesive film can also be used for this procedure as long as you are very careful to line things up properly.)

Working methodically, use the same procedure to attach all the folios in pairs, one after another. Then do the same to attach pairs of joined folios until the block of pages is one complete unit. It may take some practice to produce a text block that is even and square.

PREPARING THE SPINE AND COVERS
First, cut a piece of book board for the spine that is about $^1/_4$ inch (0.6 cm) taller and $^1/_8$ inch (0.3 cm) wider than the thickness of the text block, with the grain of the board running vertically. To accommodate a 10- × 8-inch (25- × 20-cm) text block that is 1 inch (2.5 cm) thick, for example, the spine should be $8^1/_4$ inches (21 cm) tall and $1^1/_8$ inch (2.9 cm) wide. Now cut a piece of book cloth about 4 inches (10 cm) wider and $1^1/_2$ inches (3.8 cm) taller than the spine board.

One spacer should be attached to the folded edge of each folio to create a thicker spine.

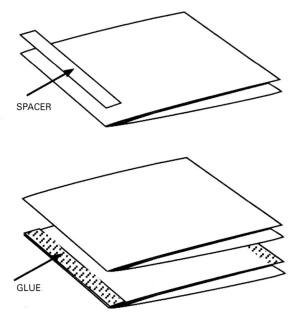

SPACER

Glue or adhesive film should be applied to the fore edge and near the fold to join each pair of folios.

GLUE

Brush glue on the spine board, place it in the center of the book cloth, and apply pressure. Flip the board and book cloth and, using a bone folder, burnish the cloth down. Flip the board over again, apply glue to the head and tail of the book cloth, and fold those flaps down (do not miter the edges). Burnish with a bone folder.

Cut two cover boards for the front and back covers, each $^1/_4$ inch (0.6 cm) taller and $^1/_8$ inch (0.3 cm) wider than the text block, with the boards' grain matching that of the spine board. Cut two strips of decorative paper, each 3 inches (7.6 cm) wide and about $1^1/_2$ inches (3.8 cm) taller than the cover boards. Apply glue to one strip and place it $1^1/_2$ inches in from the spine edge of one cover board, placing it parallel to the spine so the remaining paper hangs over the spine's edge. (Or lay the board's spine edge in the center of the glued strip.) Burnish the paper in place and then fold the paper over the head and the tail of the cover board. Apply more glue, if necessary, and wrap the other edge of the paper around the spine edge to the back of the cover board. Repeat with the other strip and cover board.

Place the spine board on your worktable with the cloth-covered side facing down, and apply glue to the long edges of the cloth, leaving $^1/_2$ inch (1.3 cm) of cloth on either side of the spine free of glue. (You can either measure and mark the gap, or use a precut $^1/_2$-inch [1.3-cm] paper strip to isolate the area to be glued.) Place the paper-lined edge of the cover board a board thickness (about $^1/_8$ inch, or 0.3 cm) away from the spine board and partially onto the glue, as shown opposite (top). Make sure that the cover board is parallel to the spine board. About $^3/_8$ inch (1 cm) of the cover board should be free of glue and unattached to the book cloth lying beneath it, as in the overhead shot of John's finished book, opposite. Attach the second cover to the other side of the spine board in the same fashion, making sure it is even and flush with the first cover. (John suggests placing the tops of the boards against a long metal straightedge to help square them to each other.)

Finally, cut two pieces of decorative paper to cover the exposed fronts of the cover boards. The paper should be large enough to provide a $^3/_4$-inch (1.9-cm) turnover on three sides of the

The spine board with one of the partially covered cover boards attached to it.

board and should overlap the spine cloth so that only about ³/₄ inch (1.9 cm) of the cloth remains exposed. Glue the paper to the boards, make well-mitered corners, burnish, and press under weight to dry.

ASSEMBLING THE BOOK

Position the text block inside the assembled cover boards and spine. (Together, the spine and cover boards are called the *case.*) Make sure the block is set evenly between the head and tail of the spine and that about ¹/₈ inch (0.3 cm) of cover board is exposed around it. Place scrap paper between the front endpaper and the first page of the text block. Apply glue to the outside of the endpaper, take a deep breath, and close the front cover board to glue it to the endpaper. (You have to believe!) Turn the book over and repeat the procedure to attach the back endpaper to the back cover. Burnish both endpapers under waxed paper to make sure they are secure and, leaving the waxed paper in place, press the book until dry.

This overhead shot of John's book shows how the double-thick pages are joined to each other but remain unattached to the spine board.

CHAPTER 3

HINGED AND EDGE-SEWN BINDINGS

H inged and edge-sewn hardcover albums can't expand to display material like accordion-fold books, or be made in a matter of minutes like some softcover journals, but they offer better protection for photos and memorabilia, and can be made with many pages to display documents or collections of paper artifacts. Once you learn the basic structures that follow, you can experiment by producing books of various sizes, punching holes in different parts of the spine to create post- or stick-bound books, or creating edge-sewn albums with decorative stitching.

Detail of double-spiral stitched bindings with hinged covers by Gail Crosman Moore. (Full image shown on page 53.)

HINGE-AND-POST BINDING

In a hinged book, the front cover (and sometimes the back cover as well) consists of two pieces: a hinge board and a cover board. A $\frac{1}{8}$-inch (0.3-cm) gap between these two pieces allows the book to open.

The technique that follows is for a hinged book that will last for years without showing wear: The hinge area of the book (which takes most of the abuse of opening and closing) is covered with sturdy paper-lined book cloth and the book is held together with screw posts. Alternatively, the hinge area can be covered with paper instead of book cloth, and the binding can be sewn, or bound with ties or sticks instead of screw posts. These variations will be discussed on page 46.

BASIC TECHNIQUE

For this post-bound version of the hinged book, the steps have been divided into four basic stages: preparing and covering the hinge, applying the cover papers, creating the text block, and assembling the book.

PREPARING AND COVERING THE HINGE

First, determine the shape and size of the book you'd like to make. Cut four pieces of book board (two for the front and back covers and two hinge pieces), making sure the grain of the board

runs vertically. The hinge boards should be at least 1 inch (2.5 cm) wide; make yours as wide as desired to coordinate with the size of your book. You must also factor in a $\frac{1}{8}$-inch (0.3-cm) gap between the hinge board and the cover board. This gap allows the book to open at the hinge. As an example, the book pictured at left measures $8\frac{3}{8} \times 6\frac{3}{4}$ inches (21.3×17.1 cm). The front and back cover boards each measure $7 \times 6\frac{3}{4}$ inches (17.8×17.1 cm), and each hinge board measures $1\frac{1}{4} \times 6\frac{3}{4}$ inches (3.2×17.1 cm). You can also choose to make the book with a hinged front cover and a one-piece back cover, but make sure you allow for the $\frac{1}{8}$-inch (0.3-cm) gap when calculating the overall width of the back cover.

Cut four pieces of paper-backed book cloth. Two pieces should each be $1\frac{1}{2}$ inches (3.8 cm) taller (to allow for a $\frac{3}{4}$-inch [1.9-cm] turnover) and 2 inches (5 cm) wider than a hinge board. The other two pieces should be $\frac{1}{4}$ inch (0.6 cm) shorter and 1 inch (2.5 cm) wider than a hinge board.

Apply glue to a hinge board and place it, glue-side down, on one of the larger pieces of book cloth. A $\frac{3}{4}$-inch (2-cm) margin of cloth should

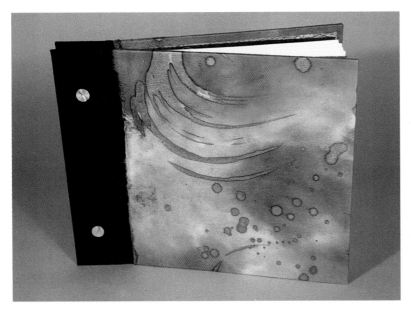

A hinged, post-bound scrapbook covered in batik paper, made by Tom Hollander.

extend from the top, bottom, and left-hand edges of the board, with a 1¼-inch (3.2-cm) margin on the right-hand edge. Flip the hinge and cloth over and burnish to smooth out the glued area. Turn them wrong-side up again and place over a piece of scrap paper. Miter the corners along the left edge of the cloth by cutting them on a diagonal.

Place the balsa or Plexiglas spacer on the margin of cloth to the right of the hinge board, then apply glue to the end of one cover board. Press the cover board in place next to the spacer, lining it up flush with the hinge board. (If you are not using a spacer, measure and place the cover board about ⅛ inch [0.3 cm] away from the hinge board, as shown in the picture below.) To determine how much glue to spread along the end of

the cover board, place it next to the spacer and draw pencil lines on the board's head and tail to mark where the book cloth ends. Apply glue up to these marks, then press the board in place.

Remove the spacer and brush a bit of glue into the gap. Flip the cloth-covered boards and, using a bone folder, burnish the boards and smooth the book cloth into the hinge groove.

Flip the boards again and apply glue to all edges of the book cloth, as well as to the lips of the cover boards as you run your brush along them. Starting with the head and tail, fold over the cloth flaps and burnish them in place. Miter the corners, using a bit more glue if necessary. Be sure to burnish the hinge groove on the inside of the book, too, as shown below.

Placing the cover board flush with the hinge board on the book cloth. Note the wooden spacer, a handy assist for board placement.

Folding over the book cloth at the head of the book.

Using a bone folder to make a neatly mitered corner at the spine of the book.

Using a bone folder to press the glue-covered book cloth into the hinge groove.

Gluing book cloth in place to line the hinge.

Applying decorative paper to one of the glued cover boards.

Burnishing down the folded-over flap at the head of the book.

Brush glue onto one of the smaller pieces of book cloth and lightly position it inside the hinge board you just covered, to line it (shown at left). Notice that part of the cloth should extend onto the inside of the cover board. Bend the hinge of the book toward and away from you to mimic the action of opening the cover; this will move the glued cloth slightly away from the cover board, ensuring that the hinge has the necessary "give" for proper functioning of the book. When the cloth is properly positioned, burnish it down, running the bone folder into the hinge groove as you work.

Repeat the whole process to create a hinged back cover, unless you have opted for a one-piece back.

APPLYING THE COVER PAPERS

Cut two pieces of decorative paper for wrapping the cover boards. Each piece should have a vertical grain direction and be $1^1/2$ inches (3.8 cm) taller and $1/2$ inch (1.3 cm) wider than the cover board (not including the hinge board), allowing for a $3/4$-inch (1.9-cm) turnover on three sides. (Because the book cloth extends onto the cover board, the decorative paper should begin about $1/4$ inch [0.6 cm] in from the left edge of the board.) If you are making a one-piece back cover, the paper should be $1^1/2$ inches (3.8 cm) taller and $1^1/2$ inches wider than the back cover board.

Start with the front cover board. Measure about $1/4$ inch (0.6 cm) to the right of the hinge groove (away from the spine and toward the fore edge of the book) and pencil a faint positioning line on the book cloth. Working over scrap paper, brush glue onto the front of the exposed cover board and very lightly onto the narrow section of book cloth to the right of your positioning line. Apply the cover paper to the pasted board as shown at left (middle), overlapping the pencil line slightly and making sure that the paper extends at least $3/4$ inch (1.9 cm) over the top, bottom, and fore edge of the board. Burnish the paper in place. Flip the cover over and miter the corners. Apply glue to the top and bottom paper flaps, fold them over, and burnish them down (shown at left). Then glue, fold over, and burnish the side flap in place, making neatly folded corners.

Cut a piece of text-weight paper $1/2$ inch (1.3 cm) shorter and $1/2$ inch (1.3 cm) narrower than the cover board (not including the hinge board) to line the inside of the cover board, as shown at right. Apply glue to the paper, working from the center outward. Center one end of the paper, glue-side down, $1/4$ inch (0.6 cm) in from the spine edge of the exposed cover board. Use the bone folder to smooth it down toward the right edge and burnish in place to finish. Encase the finished book cover in waxed paper and press overnight or until dry.

Repeat the entire process to cover the back.

CREATING THE TEXT BLOCK

Cut or tear 20 to 24 cover-weight pages to use for the interior of the book. Each page should be $1/2$ inch (1.3 cm) shorter and $1/4$ inch (0.6 cm) narrower than the cover boards. This allows for a $1/4$-inch (0.6-cm) margin on three sides when the pages are aligned with the spine edge of the covers. Add spacers between the pages to thicken the spine edge of the text block and allow the book to lie flat when photos are added (see page 24 and tip, below). Spacers can be made from the same cover-weight material as the book pages; they should be as wide as the hinge board and as tall as the page. Use a glue stick to tack them in

place on the spine edge of each page so as to keep them in position during drilling.

ASSEMBLING THE BOOK

Make a paper template the same size as the hinge board for marking where the spine holes should go. Draw a line down the center of the template and make two marks on the line that are equidistant from the top and bottom edges of the template, as shown in the illustration on page 46.

The inside of the book cover with its paper liner in place.

TIP

Here's an alternate way to make spacers: Make the page and spacer in one piece. To do this, measure your back cover (including the hinge board) and subtract $1/2$ inch (1.3 cm) from its height and $1/4$ inch (0.6 cm) from its width to get the measurement for the finished page. Then add 1 inch (2.5 cm) to the page width and cut or tear a number of pages to this oversize measurement. Using a square and a bone folder or awl, score each page 1 inch (2.5 cm) in from the left-hand side. Fold the page *away* from the score line to create the attached spacer.

Scoring pages to create attached spacers.

TIP

If you want
to conceal the
screw posts,
fold the hinges
on the front
and back covers
inside the book
to hold the
paper. In this
style, which is
popular commer-
cially, a much
larger gap must
be left between
the hinge and
the cover boards
to allow for the
turned hinge.

I usually place my holes 1 1/4 inch (3.2 cm) in from the book's head and tail, but you can place them wherever you prefer. Gather and align the text pages and spacers and center them, flush with the spine, between the book covers. Clamp them together with the template on top of the stack. Check whether the screw posts are long enough to accommodate the pages you've assembled, and add or subtract pages and spacers if necessary.

Work over several pieces of scrap or conventional book board and, if drilling holes, use a clamp to stabilize the book by attaching it to a table. Be sure to choose the correct size bit (usually 1/4 inch or 0.6 cm) for your electric or hand drill so that your screw posts fit snugly. If punching holes, use the template to mark where holes should be made in the covers. After punching holes through the cover, center one page spacer below the cover to mark where the page holes should be punched. Use that spacer as a page hole template, clamping it over stacks of pages and spacers to mark the exact position for repeated punching with a screw punch or a rubber mallet and punch set.

Assemble the book by lining up the holes in the cover and pages and inserting the screw posts, tightening them to hold the book together.

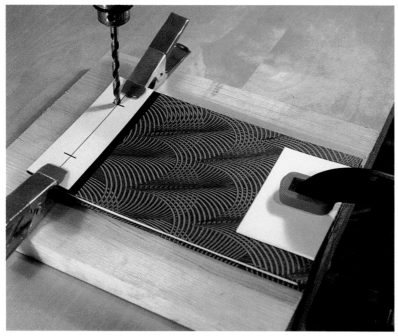

The book covers, pages, and spacers clamped together with a hole template on top, in preparation for drilling.

VARIATIONS: HINGE-AND-STICK OR HINGE-AND-TIE BINDINGS

You can vary the hinged book by using ties or sticks, rather than screw posts, to bind the book, and paper, rather than book cloth, to wrap the hinge area. These alternate versions can be made quite easily but, because the hinge grooves will be less sturdy, are not the best for books that will get heavy use. An album holding pictures of wedding cakes to be shown to prospective clients several times a week, for example, would need a sturdier hinge. But if you choose a strong and flexible cover material, such as a thick handmade paper, and reinforce the gap between the hinge and the front cover board, you can make an album that will be reasonably strong and will function well as a home for ticket stubs and reviews of your favorite films.

To make one of these books, cut a front hinge board and cover board as described on page 42. For the back cover, cut only a single piece of board, making sure that the grain runs vertically. The combined width of the hinge piece, the 1/8-inch (0.3-cm) gap, and the front cover should equal the width of the one-piece back cover.

Position the hinge and front cover board 1/8 inch (0.3 cm) apart and apply linen or framer's hinging tape over the gap between them, tucking it into the groove with a bone folder. Wrap both the hinged front cover and single-piece back cover with decorative paper, each piece 1 1/2 inches (3.8 cm) taller and 1 1/2 inches (3.8 cm) wider than the back cover to allow a 3/4-inch (1.9-cm) margin of paper on all four sides. Miter all four corners of both covers, glue down the flaps, and burnish to finish.

Line both covers with text-weight decorative or plain paper as before, making sure that the grain runs vertically to match that of the cover papers and boards. Each piece of paper should be 1/2 inch (1.3 cm) shorter and narrower than the back cover, allowing a 1/4-inch (0.6-cm) margin all around. Wrap the covers in waxed paper and press until dry.

Cut pages and spacers from cover-weight paper or card stock and attach as before. Gather and align the pages, clamp at the spine, and drill or punch spine holes. Tie the book closed as explained for the simple tied binding (page 24), using ribbon, cord, or raffia. Alternatively, use a rubber-band-and-stick binding as explained on page 25.

Stick-bound variations of the hinged cover design with paper-covered hinges and cover boards, by Claudia Lee. For a sturdier album, the hinge area should be covered with book cloth.

TIP

Rather than covering the hinge board and front cover board together as one piece, you can also try covering them separately, as though they were accordion-book covers. Then simply position the two pieces ⅛ inch (0.3 cm) apart on a piece of strong, flexible endpaper and secure with glue. The endpaper, which should be as tall and as wide as both parts of the cover combined, including the ⅛-inch (0.3-cm) gap, will effectively line the boards and provide the hinge for the book. (Because it is sturdier, it is better to use book cloth than paper as an endpaper for this type of book if it is designed for anything but minimal use.)

The hinge and front cover board wrapped separately, ready to be glued to a sturdy cloth endpaper.

EDGE-SEWN BINDINGS

Edge-sewn bindings, also known as stab bindings, employ decorative stitching patterns to hold interior pages and covers together at the spine of the book. The stitching patterns can be simple, requiring just two spine holes, or elaborate, requiring twelve or more holes. There are many variations possible, but most edge-sewn bindings share two common rules: You must sew into each stitching hole two or more times, and you must repeatedly carry your cord or thread around the outside edge of the spine (and often over the book's head and tail edges as well).

Edge-sewn bindings are an exciting way to bind either softcover or hinged hardcover books. Although it may look intimidating, you'll soon see that the steps progress quite logically. You may even start designing your own stitching patterns after creating a few of these books. I recommend cutting a few narrow pieces of mat board and punching sewing holes in them to practice new stitching patterns. My early practice boards, reminiscent of the sewing cards I had as a child, remain a handy reference today.

Doris Arndt used wire instead of the usual ribbon or cord to make the edge-sewn binding for this scrapbook.

Marbled and paste paper designs decorate the hinged covers of these edge-sewn books.

WHAT YOU'LL NEED

- Cover-weight paper for text block
- Book board for hard covers, or heavy handmade paper or decorated watercolor paper for soft covers
- Decorative paper to wrap covers (hardcover books only)
- Text-weight decorative or plain paper for endpapers (hardcover books only)
- Strong, nonstretching stitching material, like ribbon, cord, or bookbinder's thread

BASIC TECHNIQUE

Prepare the covers and text block using the basic methods already explained. (For a softcover book, see page 24; for a hinged hardcover book, see page 27.) If you make your pages the same height as the covers, you will be able to easily position them for drilling or punching multiple holes. Also note that the text block should include spacers to thicken the spine, as explained on page 24.

Choose your stitching pattern (see pages 50–53), then measure and punch the appropriate number of holes. Be sure to make the holes large enough to accommodate multiple strands, depending upon the particular design and stitching material you've chosen. For more patterns, check the Further Reading section for books devoted solely to constructing handbound books.

This softcover journal with a two-hole edge-sewn binding was inspired by the life and quick-change artistry of my chameleon. Chalk-marbled papers by Delia Quinn decorate the handmade paper cover.

This album has a two-hole edge-sewn binding and is covered in a classical marbled design.

THE TWO-HOLE BINDING

The stitching material for this binding will pass through each spine hole three times. Keeping this in mind, coordinate your choice of ribbon, braid, or strong nonstretching cord with the size of the spine holes you wish to make. The length of your stitching material should be about seven times the height of your book cover.

Align your pages and covers so they are flush at the spine edge, then drill or punch two sewing holes through your spine. I place mine 1/2 inch (1.3 cm) in from the spine edge and 1 1/4 inches

TIP

Use an awl or ball burnisher (used for embossing) to gently force ribbon or flexible cord through the punched stitching holes, if necessary. A pair of needle-nosed pliers can also be a helpful tool.

(3.2 cm) from the head and tail of the book, but they can be placed wherever you prefer. Clamp your album to keep the cover and spine holes lined up, and begin stitching as follows:

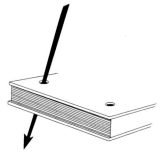

1. Enter the top hole in the front cover, leaving a tail of ribbon about 9 inches (23 cm) long to tie in a decorative bow when you're finished. If you are stitching with bookbinder's thread or embroidery floss and intend to end with a knot instead of a bow, leave a shorter tail.

2. Wrap the ribbon over the head of the book and sew back into the same hole. (Pull the ribbon taut as you stitch.)

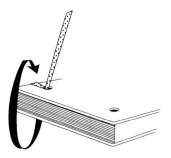

3. Sew around the spine of the book and into the hole a third time, exiting through the back cover.

4. Sew across the back cover and into the second hole at the tail end of the book.

5. Sew around the spine of the book and up through this hole a second time.

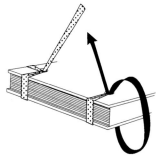

6. Wrap the ribbon over the tail edge of the book and sew up into the hole a third time, exiting through the front cover. Tie the ends of the ribbon in a bow, as shown on page 49. If you've chosen to end with a knot, knot the stitching material, then clip close to the ends and apply a tiny spot of glue to secure. You can also poke the knot and ends of thread into a sewing hole to hide them.

THE FOUR-HOLE BINDING

Although this binding may appear difficult, it is only a variation of the two-hole binding and is quite simple. Here again, the stitching material will pass through each hole three times. Keep this in mind when choosing your material and judging the size of the holes. Cut a length of cord about seven times the height of the book cover—longer if you have a very thick book, or shorter if you don't intend to leave long tails of cord.

Create four holes with a drill, awl, or hole punch, using a template to place them 1/2 inch (1.3 cm) in from the spine edge. Two of the holes can be placed about 3/4 inch (1.9 cm) in from the head and tail of the book, with the other two holes set at equal distances between them. Clamp the book and begin by following steps 1 through 3 of the two-hole binding pattern opposite. Then continue with the stitching pattern as follows:

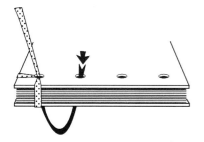

4. Sew across the back cover and up through the second hole.

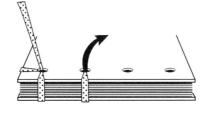

5. Sew around the spine and up through the same hole.

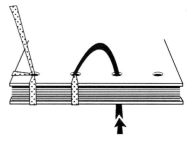

6. Sew across the front cover and down through the third hole.

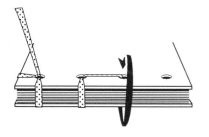

7. Sew around the spine and down through the same hole.

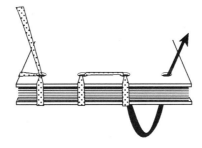

8. Sew across the back cover and up through the fourth hole.

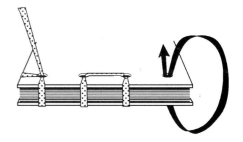

9. Sew around the tail of the book and up through the same hole.

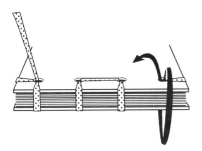

10. Sew around the spine and up through the fourth hole a third time.

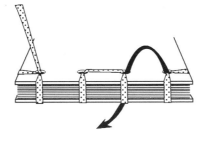

11. Sew across the front cover and down through the third hole.

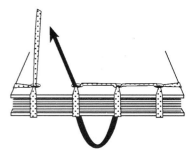

12. Sew across the back cover and up through the second hole to join the original tail of cord. Tie off the cords in a knot or bow.

EDGE-SEWN BINDINGS

This same sewing pattern can be continued for any number of holes, whether to cover the spine with more closely spaced decorative stitches or to bind taller books. You may also want to embellish the binding by adding beads or knots to the cord ends or, as in Lisa Pedolsky's book shown below, adding beads or bells to the cords as you sew. A group of travel journals by Michael Jacobs, also shown below, further illustrates this pattern's versatility for either soft- or hardcover books.

A four-hole edge-sewn binding with Indian dance bell decoration, by Lisa Pedolsky.

Some of the many softcover edge-sewn travel journals created by Michael Jacobs. PHOTO BY BILL WICKETT

THE DOUBLE-SPIRAL STITCHED BINDING

Like the four-hole binding, the double-spiral stitched binding can be adjusted to fit any number of stitching holes, again offering a wealth of creative options.

This time the cord needs to be no more than five times the height of your book cover as it will pass through each stitching hole only twice. To begin, create a column of spine holes equidistant from each other, clamp the book together, then stitch the binding as follows:

Double-spiral stitched bindings by Gail Crosman Moore. Gail uses rubber stamp and paper dyeing techniques to create decorative paper for her books.

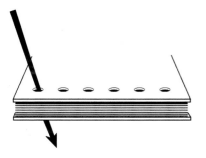

1. Stitch through the top hole in the front cover, leaving a tail of cord.

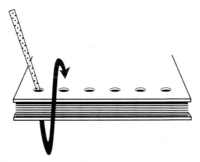

2. Wrap around the spine edge and spiral down through the second hole on the front cover.

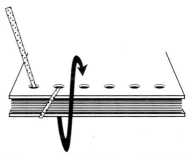

3. Wrap around the spine, and spiral down through the third hole.

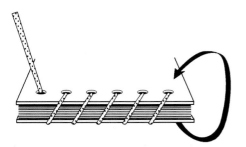

4. Continue stitching and spiraling until you get to the last hole. Enter this hole, wrap around the tail of the book, and stitch back through the same hole.

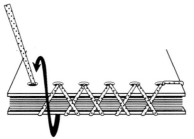

5. Spiral back up the spine of the album, with each stitch wrapping around the spine edge.

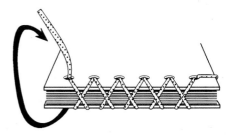

6. After you enter the last hole, wrap the cord around the head of the book and tie it to the original tail of cord.

CHAPTER 4

INNOVATIVE COVERS AND PAGES

Now that you've learned how to construct books using various types of bindings, it's time to decorate the covers and pages with innovative paper art techniques that will showcase your photos and memorabilia. The suggestions in this chapter won't be appropriate if you want to slip your scrapbooks and photo albums neatly into a bookshelf next to other books. But if you want to create albums that are works of art and have cover decoration worthy of constant display, read on.

Detail of a woven design used to decorate a hardcover book. (Full image shown in weaving section, on page 70.)

WORKING WITH COLOR

Choosing colors that complement each other is important no matter what type of artwork you do, and as you create designs for your covers and pages you'll need to make numerous decisions regarding color. Your own color preference can of course dominate, but with some knowledge of how colors are created and interact with each other, you can more easily create a composition that is harmonious and striking rather than boring or jarring.

If you don't have experience mixing colors, spend a little time studying a color wheel, like the one shown opposite. The three primary colors—red, blue, and yellow—can be mixed in pairs to yield three secondary colors—purple, orange, and green (for example, blue + yellow = green). The six tertiary colors are made by mixing a primary color with its adjacent secondary color (for example, blue + green = blue-green). Your color palette can be further extended by tinting colors with white or shading them with black to make them darker or lighter. Note that in a composition, dark colors will appear to recede, while lighter ones will advance.

Another factor to consider when choosing a color palette is the *temperature* of your colors. Cool colors like blue, green, and purple—colors that remind us of mountains or oceans—appear to

TIP

In addition to being used on your handmade books, many of the cover decorating techniques that follow can be adapted for use on inexpensive purchased albums made of heavy book board. The transformation will amaze you.

If the book, like most, has a removable double-wire spiral binding, you can open the binding, remove the covers, and either decorate the book boards or wrap them with decorative paper. If you've adhered paper to the boards, press them until dry. Then either punch holes through the paper over the existing holes in the spine or, if the holes are square, recut them with an X-acto knife. Then reattach the spiral binding wire.

Hélène Métivier removed the cover from a spiral-bound album and decorated it with stamping, direct pigment-to-paper techniques (see caption, page 99), and layered mats to create this feline-themed photo album.

A color wheel shows how the three primary colors—red, blue, and yellow—can be mixed to yield a range of hues.

recede in a composition, while warm colors like red, orange, and yellow leap forward like the flames they suggest.

Although this information may seem more applicable to painters than book artists, some knowledge of color theory can be quite helpful for bookmaking. It can, for example, prevent you from choosing a background paper that will overpower a photo to be placed on that page. It can also prevent your collage from becoming a mad jumble of colors and textures.

Four harmonious color schemes to experiment with are as follows:

- *Monochromatic:* tints and shades of a single color, such as light, medium, and dark green
- *Analogous:* colors adjacent to each other on the color wheel, such as blue, blue-green, and green
- *Complementary:* one primary color and the secondary color that lies opposite it on the color

wheel, such as blue and orange. These combinations create the highest contrast.
- *Triadic:* three colors spaced equidistant on the color wheel, such as red, blue, and yellow

Other ideas for color schemes can be derived by looking around you at colors in nature to see how they complement each other; I often refer to the colors in my flower garden when choosing palettes. Also pay attention to wrapping paper and fabric designs, and look through art books, magazines, and upscale mail-order catalogs to see what kinds of color combinations you prefer.

Try making a scrapbook of color combinations you like. Let one hue dominate each page and add colored ribbons, paint chip samples, and colored paper swatches to photos you've cut from magazines. You'll learn about color harmony, composition, and your personal color preferences as you create your scrapbook, which is sure to be a lasting and valuable resource for all your artistic pursuits.

COLLAGE

Gluing materials to scrapbook or album covers and pages is a great way to decorate them. The elements can be just a few ticket stubs, seed packets, coins, or other artifacts neatly arranged within a beautiful border or frame, or they can be all manner of paper ephemera designed to spill over your cover or page in an abstract design.

MATERIALS

Finding collage materials is not difficult. Materials for the cover can have a good deal of relief, so even things like your great-grandmother's sewing scissors, your very first car key, or your lucky Monopoly piece can be used to reflect a theme or create a feeling related to the interior of your book.

Janet Hofacker, an artist who describes her collages as "scavenger art," finds many of her materials lying in city streets. Many of us don't even have to leave the house to find materials: We just naturally save stuff. If you can remember where you've stashed it, you may have a great base on which to build a storehouse of collage materials. Sewing baskets often contain old tassels, strips of lace, and interesting buttons that can be incorporated into a work, along with strips of leather or fabric on which to place them. Your jewelry box may yield old pins, solo earrings, or charms that no longer have a bracelet to call home. Feathers, sea glass, small shells, and twigs saved from nature walks may be lurking in desk drawers or in cigar boxes tucked away in the attic. Imagine my surprise

A collaged album page with rubber stamp art, made by Roberta Altshuler.

when a friend recently suggested I use some groundhog vertebrae he'd found on such a walk. Pretty horrific, until I noticed that the vertebrae made great beads. Garages and basement workshops can provide you with wire, string, brass washers, and other interesting metal treasures. If you've already discarded all these things (probably yesterday), don't despair: Antique shops, flea markets, and auctions can quickly refill your larder.

Paper materials also make excellent collage elements, including old photos, negatives and contact sheets, scraps of wallpaper, playbills, ticket stubs, postcards, blueprints, sales tickets, boarding passes, maps, sheet music, menus from foreign restaurants, stamps, and so on. Acidic papers should be photocopied or coated with a matte medium to extend their lifespan. (For more information about working with acidic papers, see page 17.) Decorative papers and handmade papers that you've made or purchased can be cut, torn, dyed, stamped, colored with paints or inks, crumpled, corrugated, marbled, stenciled, and so on. Many artists alter their collages by sanding and peeling back the surface of the paper, or wire brushing it, to make it appear old, weather-beaten, or distressed. Some, like Janet Hofacker, use structural paints, sealing wax, and cloth to add dimension and texture.

TIP

If the idea of creating a collage on a book you've spent hours creating leaves you wincing, retreat to a position of safety by creating your collage on a piece of heavy paper, as if you were making a greeting card. When it is dry, attach the finished collage to your book cover. No one will know you were faint of heart, especially if the base paper has a decorative edge. The book shown here was created especially to receive one of Lea Everse's beautiful collaged cards on its cover.

An accordion-fold book by Lea Everse.

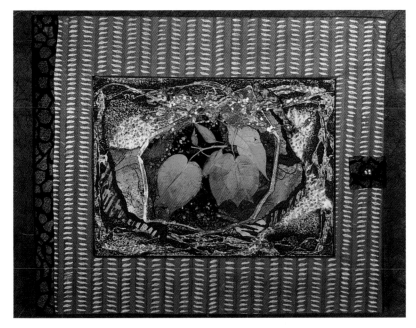

On this album cover, created by Susan Pickering Rothamel, pressed flowers and gold mica flakes are sandwiched between thin layers of mica tile. Susan creates exciting cover collages by combining a number of art materials, some of which she produces through her company USArtQuest, Inc. Here, additional effects were created by using copper foil tape, handmade paper, embossing powders, and more metallic flakes melted onto heat-resistant tape.

Sherrill Kahn, whose work is pictured below, used acrylic paints and sponging techniques to transform common paper towels into collage materials. She often uses pieces of Play-Doh as additional accents in her work.

Sherrill Kahn transformed lowly paper towels into stunning collage materials for this journal cover.

BASIC TECHNIQUES

There are two rules that apply to any collage, whether it's a large one to be framed or a small design for a scrapbook cover or page: First, repeated shapes and colors will help unify a design and keep your eye moving through it. And second, some contrast—a diagonal line in a mainly horizontal design, a rough corrugated paper next to smooth ones, a flash of intense color—will keep the collage exciting.

Whether you are making a wildly abstract collage or a highly structured one, its a good idea to first lay out your design on a book board cut to the same size as your book cover, to see how the composition looks. This way you can overlap papers in different ways, move elements around, and rotate materials to create horizontal and vertical structures. Look at other collages on card fronts, book covers, and in art books to see what you find aesthetically pleasing. Then let your intuition guide you. If it's a really complicated design, I usually take a Polaroid photograph of it so I can re-create it piece by piece as I glue the elements in place.

To attach lightweight collage papers to your book covers and pages, use an acrylic matte medium, which will also give the papers a protective coating. I also like to use "Yes" Paste as it won't wrinkle papers. PVA glues can also be used, but too much will wrinkle thinner stock and may cause

A picture of my grandparents and articles from my grandmother's sewing basket decorate this watercolor-paper scrapbook page.

some buckling on a cover that, if it has dimension, can't be pressed again. Be sparing in your use of adhesives for holding heavier materials like metals and wood, to avoid unsightly accumulations of glue.

Collages can also be sewn together, either by hand or machine. Artist Claudia Lee, whose machine-stitched work is shown at right, often uses a decorative topstitch that adds yet another design element to her work. She then glues her finished collage to the cover of a book. Sometimes Claudia continues the stitching to create a stitched paper border around the edges of a softcover book. Stitching can also be used to create fabric or paper quilts, which work beautifully as covers for scrapbooks of favorite paste-paper, marbled, or orizomegami designs (all discussed in Chapter 5).

To make a glued paper quilt, which is much less time-consuming than stitching one, draw the design on a piece of book board and then cut quilting squares and triangles to fit. Secure the pieces with glue or adhesive film, which will make the piecing go quickly. You can use any number of purchased decorative papers or make your own quilt pieces by using some of the paper decorating techniques in Chapter 5. You can also cover the book board with a solid-colored decorative paper first, then lay the quilt pieces near each other, using the solid borders between them as decorative accents. Another option is to make a kind of "crazy quilt" by overlapping the pieces. Check quilting books to find patterns for traditional designs, or modify them to come up with your own.

Above: Claudia Lee often assembles her collages by machine-stitching them together, then glues the finished collage to her book cover.

Left: Jennifer Philippoff cut art posters into triangles and rearranged the pieces in a crazy quilt design to create this book cover.

WINDOWS

By cutting a window in a book's front cover board or paper, a space can be isolated to focus attention on an object or decorative accent, like a slice of a geode or a quilled design. The hardcover accordion book pictured below was designed to display pictures of vintage planes taken at an air show, with the window created to show off a small vintage toy airplane. Windows can be added to almost any type of book, whether hardcover or softcover. Here, instructions are given for creating a rectangular, 3- × 2¼-inch (7.6- × 5.7-cm) window for the cover of a small 7- × 7-inch (17.8- × 17.8-cm) accordion-fold album. They can be adjusted to create windows in any size album.

A photo album designed to hold photos of an air show. The window in the front cover displays a small vintage toy airplane.

WHAT YOU'LL NEED

- Mat board for front cover
- Book board for back cover
- Decorative text-weight paper for wrapping covers
- Decorative text-weight paper for background of window. If making a softcover book, use cover-weight paper.

BASIC TECHNIQUE

Because it is difficult to cut a window in thick binder's board, the front cover of this project will be made with a piece of mat board or a similar weight book board, which will eventually be laminated to another piece of mat board. The back cover will not contain a window, so it can be made from a single piece of heavier board. (If you don't mind a book with thinner covers, windowed albums can, of course, be made with mat board only.)

TIP

The directions given here can be modified for adding windows to hinged hard covers or soft covers. When working with laminated hinged covers containing windows, make sure that both sections of the front cover are the same thickness. You don't want your cover to end up thicker at one end than the other, which will present a problem if covering it with a single piece of decorative paper. For softcover books, the front endpaper can be used to support the window liner or, if it is heavy enough and double sided, like many decorative handmade papers, can serve as the liner itself.

CUTTING THE WINDOW

Start by cutting two 7- × 7-inch (17.8- × 17.8-cm) pieces of mat board for the front cover and one 7- × 7-inch (17.8- × 17.8-cm) piece of heavier book board for the back cover, with the grain running vertically on all pieces. (Ideally, the back cover will be about the same thickness as the two pieces of mat board combined.)

If you're not sure where to place the window in your cover, cut a piece of paper the size of the window and move it around on the cover to get an idea of how various positions will look. A centering ruler with a zero as the center mark will come in handy for making sure margins around the window are even. Otherwise use a conventional square to measure and draw four intersecting lines to determine window placement.

Prepare to cut a 3-inch-wide (7.6-cm-wide) window in the center of one of the pieces of mat board by subtracting the width of the window (3 inches/7.6 cm) from the width of the board (7 inches/17.8 cm). In this example, 7 − 3 = 4 inches (or 17.8 − 7.6 = 10.2 cm). Then divide your answer in half to determine how far in from either edge of the board you should draw vertical cutting lines. Here, 4 ÷ 2 = 2 inches (or 10.2 ÷ 2 = 5.1 cm), so you would draw your lines 2 inches (5.1 cm) from each edge.

Now decide how far down from the top of the board you want the window to begin. Usually, an amount equal to the space on either side of the window is chosen. Draw a horizontal cutting line at this point and extend it to intersect with the vertical cutting lines. Draw another horizontal line 2¼ inches (5.7 cm) below the first to create a rectangle the height and width of your window. Using a square and mat knife, cut out the window.

ADDING DECORATIVE PAPER

To wrap the windowed front cover, cut out a piece of decorative paper 2 inches (5 cm) wider and taller than the cover. Apply glue to one side of the windowed cover and place it, glue-side down, in the center of the decorative paper. Turn the cover over, burnish it down, then flip it over again to expose the uncovered mat board. Use an X-acto knife to cut diagonal slits (an "x") in the windowed area, ending each line just a hair away from the corner of the window. Cut out the center of the slit area to create flat-edged paper flaps, then apply glue and fold the window flaps over to the inside of the cover, as shown above right. Burnish the flaps down.

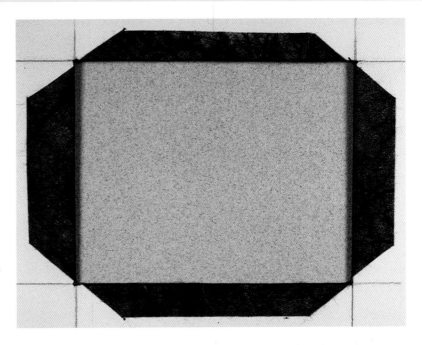

Decorative paper will also be used to create a liner for the window, which will serve as an attractive backdrop for the featured object. Glue and burnish down a 3-inch-square (7.6-cm-square) piece of decorative paper or fabric in the center of the second piece of mat board. If you are making a larger or smaller window, modify the liner's dimensions so that they are the correct size. Also, if you did not cut your window in the center of the first board, make sure you adjust placement of the liner on the second board so it falls exactly below the windowed opening.

Apply glue to the back of the windowed cover and glue it in position on top of the second piece of mat board. Be sure that the edges line up exactly. Miter the corners of the decorative cover paper (which should should still be untrimmed on the windowed mat board) and apply adhesive to the paper flaps. Fold the flaps over both pieces of mat board at once and burnish them down.

Create the back cover and text block by following the instructions on page 32. (If you are not making an accordion-fold book, follow the directions appropriate for the type of book you are making.) Then press the finished book until dry. As a final step, glue the decorative object in place in the windowed opening.

An inverted book cover with window flaps glued in place.

VARIATIONS: CIRCULAR AND RECESSED WINDOWS

The directions on pages 62–63 can be easily modified to create other types of windows. To make a circular window, use a compass cutter or other device made for cutting circular openings

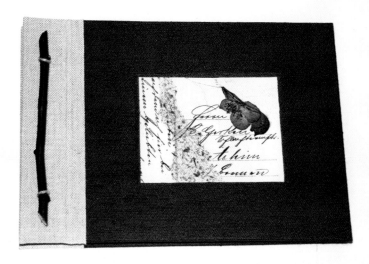

The recessed window in this stick-bound book by Deborah Waimon contains one of Deborah's collages.

A paper mat cut from heavy fibrous handmade paper makes the perfect window for the label on this album of hot sauce recipes.

in mat board. Cut a circular opening of the desired size in your mat board, then cover the board with decorative paper, as before. Flip the board over and cut a crude circle about 1/2 inch (1.3 cm) smaller than the circular opening in the mat board, then cut slits every 1/4 inch (0.6 cm) to facilitate smooth folding of the paper flaps. Apply glue to each tiny flap and fold it individually around the mat board, forming a circle. Then continue as before to finish the book.

Another variation involves creating a depression in a hard cover to showcase a paper or object, as on Deborah Waimon's cover, shown at left. This time, use an X-acto knife to score an area on the front of a piece of book board and then lift off some of the layers of paper, or "ply," that make up the board. Cover the book board with paper or cloth, then use your fingers to outline the area of the depression. Cut x-shaped slits in the cloth or paper spanning the depression and, using a bone folder, ease the material down onto the depressed area, burnishing it up against the edges of the window you've created. Then cut a paper or photo to glue into the depression.

An easy raised window can be created by covering a precut mat with the same paper or fabric used to wrap a hard cover. Once the mat has been covered, the window opened, and all the paper flaps adhered to the back of the mat, you can glue it in place over a drawing or photo on the front of a finished album. You can even place a sheet of Mylar below the mat to form a window for pressed flowers.

Heavy decorative or handmade papers can also be cut into mats and applied to your hard- or softcover books to create borders for cover decorations, as on my album of hot sauce recipes, shown at left. Mats can be cut from purchased corrugated paper and layered with other papers, or cut from corrugated paper you've made with a paper crimper. (Fiskars makes a good one.) The edges of lighter-weight papers can be cut with edging scissors or given a deckle edge for added interest. (See page 19 for information on creating deckle edges.)

OTHER DESIGN ELEMENTS

A number of other craft techniques can be used to decorate the covers and pages of your books. Some, like making rolled paper tube and quilled designs, can add considerable dimension to your work. Others, like weaving and metal piercing, are perfect ways to add interest to ready-made purchased books or plain covers you've made yourself. Finally, using pressed leaves and flowers as accents or the focal point on covers and pages can introduce a nostalgic or romantic theme.

PAPER TUBES

You can compose a strikingly different book cover by creating a mat from rolled paper tubes, like the one shown below. The rolled design pictured was created on a custom-cut mat and then glued to a finished accordion-style album that housed photos of Indonesian craftsmen. The colors and tubes on the cover complement bamboo, which is seen in many of the photos. Other papers and arrangements of tubes could be used for different themes, such as an art deco design for a scrapbook of 1920s memorabilia.

The technique is simple. Just choose a paper that's thin enough to roll, then cut it into strips with an X-acto knife and metal rule. (Zachary Vaughn, who created the work shown, usually starts with strips that measure 3×5 inches [7.6×13 cm].) Roll each strip around a pencil or dowel to form a tube and glue the edge in place. If you want a thinner tube, roll the paper around a needle or thin rod. Line the tubes up on waxed paper to keep them from sticking to your work surface. When the glue is dry, remove the paper supports and begin gluing the tubes to a purchased precut mat (or one you've created) that's been wrapped in decorative paper to match the book cover.

You may want to sketch out your design first, then cut and roll tubes to fit, or even draw positioning marks on the mat before gluing the tubes in place. If you do need to trim some tubes to keep corners square, use a sharp pair of scissors to snip off the ends and then reinsert paper supports to reshape any dented tubes. When the design is complete and glued in place on the mat, use adhesive film to adhere the mat to the book cover. (You won't be able to press this book.)

A rolled paper tube design by Zachary Vaughn creates an unusual book cover for this album, which contains photos of Indonesian crafts.

INDONESIAN CRAFTS

QUILLING

Another type of paper rolling, known as quilling or paper filigree, is done by rolling narrow strips of paper into coiled shapes and then gluing the shapes together to form intricate designs. Although rolled paper is very strong, quilled designs look rather delicate and can be used to create romantic cover designs for wedding photo albums or scrapbooks of old love letters or Victorian greeting cards. When created with thin $1/16$-inch (0.2-cm) paper strips, like the one shown opposite by Mary Anne Landfield, they have low enough relief to be used for interior pages as well.

WHAT YOU'LL NEED

- *Quilling paper.* Packs of precut quilling paper, which comes in strips approximately 24 inches (61 cm) long and $1/8$ to $1/4$ inch (0.3 to 0.6 cm) wide, and in an array of colors, are inexpensive and widely available in craft and art supply shops. If you need a particular color, want a thinner strip, or simply like to work from scratch, you can also cut your own strips with a paper cutter or X-acto knife and metal rule. A wide range of papers can be quilled, from Canson Mi-Teintes drawing paper to thin typing paper. Just make sure your paper is pliable enough to roll easily and spring open, yet has enough body to hold a quilled shape.
- *Tweezers*
- *Quilling tool.* Paper can be coiled around many types of implements, including round toothpicks, large needles, hat pins, thin dowels, and even bird feather quills (thought to be the original paper support). Thinner tools, of course, will produce coils with smaller diameters. If you have difficulty creating consistent shapes with a makeshift tool, you may find that investing in a purchased tool with a narrow shank and substantial handle makes rolling paper easier. Avoid tools with a paper slot in one end that, while they may speed up the rolling process, will leave a crimp in the center of each quilled shape.
- *Washers (optional).* Metal or rubber washers with various diameters can be used to make sure coils expand to the same size before they're glued.
- *Quilling board and straight pins.* A piece of foam core covered with a sheet of graph paper will quickly create a gridded quilling board for lining up and measuring quilled pieces. Cover the board with a piece of waxed paper to prevent glued pieces from sticking, and use straight pins to hold designs in place before gluing them together.

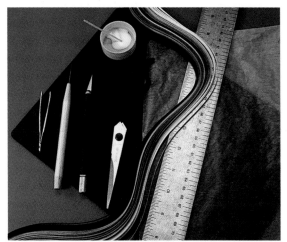

Some of the supplies used in quilling. If you purchase precut quilling strips, you won't need the X-acto knife or self-healing cutting mat.

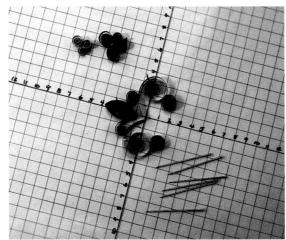

A piece of foam core covered with graph paper can be used as a quilling board to help make symmetrical designs. Mark off a grid on the graph paper to help center designs, and use straight pins to hold quilled shapes in position.

BASIC TECHNIQUE

The basic element of any quilled design is the coil, which is either open or closed. In a closed coil, the outside end is glued down and the coil is secured. In an open coil, sometimes called a scroll, the end remains unsecured and the coil is free to relax and expand.

To roll a closed coil with a purchased or improvised quilling tool, first tear off a 4-inch (10-cm) strip of quilling paper. Holding the tool as shown below, wind the cut end of the strip behind and around the tool. Use your thumb and forefinger to roll the paper toward you, applying even pressure so that each round stacks neatly on top of the last. If you're using a toothpick or thin dowel, you may find that the tool's wood snags the paper enough to help start the coil. By rotating the toothpick toward you as you work, you can sometimes use it to support and coil the paper at the same time.

Continue quilling until you've rolled the entire strip of paper, then remove the coil from your tool and let it expand slightly. Apply a dot of glue to the torn edge and hold the glued edge in place for a moment to glue it down, closing the coil.

The following are directions for some basic closed coil designs (illustrated on page 68):

- *Peg:* Roll a tight coil and glue the end down *before* removing it from the quilling tool.
- *Loose coil:* Roll a loose coil, remove it from the tool, and let it expand a bit before gluing the end down.
- *Eye-shaped coil:* Gently pinch both sides of a loose coil.
- *Leaf shape:* Bend the ends of an eye-shaped coil.
- *Teardrop:* Pinch one side of a loose coil.
- *Petal:* Bend one edge of the teardrop.

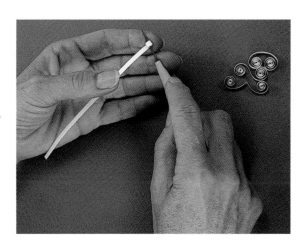

Rolling a coil.

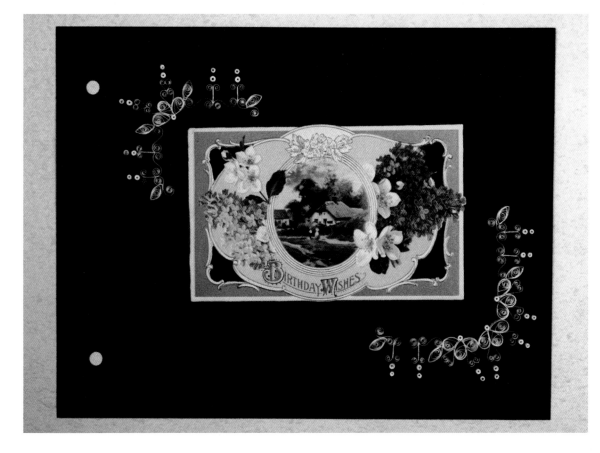

A quilled design by Mary Anne Landfield decorates this page from a scrapbook of antique postcards.

- *Triangle:* Using even pressure, pinch three sides of a loose coil.
- *Half-moon:* Press down on top of a loose coil to flatten and slightly indent it.
- *Tulip:* Indent a loose coil by pressing down in two areas.

Open coils and scrolls are rolled exactly like closed coils, except that you don't glue the ends down. Note that if both ends of your open coils are to remain exposed in a quilled work, you'll want to cut, rather than tear, the quilling paper.

Here are directions for the more basic open coil and scroll designs (illustrated below, right):

- *Loose open coil:* Roll a coil and let it spring open.
- *S-shaped scroll:* Roll one half of a strip into a coil, then turn the strip over and roll the other half.
- *Full scroll:* Roll two coils, starting at opposite ends of the paper strip.
- *V-scroll:* Crease the paper strip in the middle before rolling a full scroll toward the "mountain" side of the crease.
- *Heart scroll:* Crease the strip in the middle and roll a full scroll toward the "valley" side of the crease.

Practice making coils of different shapes and sizes. Work with paper strips that range from 2 to 8 inches (5 to 20 cm) long to get a feeling for how different sized coils are made. Also, experiment by using different colors to coordinate with your books and by varying the tightness of your coils.

To make a quilled design, join various coils and scrolls together. Some quillers like to make multiple coils in various shapes and then move the pieces around until they find a pleasing arrangement. More methodical craftspeople prefer to draw a pattern and make quilled pieces to fit. Regardless of which method you choose, be sure to work over waxed paper so that when pieces are positioned you can apply glue and assemble them.

If your design is complicated, place your pattern on a quilling board and pin each element in place before gluing. If you're creating a quilled frame to be placed around a photograph or other piece of memorabilia, note the dimensions of the item by tracing its outline on the graph paper. Then make your quilled frame to fit. When your quilled design is dry, check to see that all joins are complete. Apply tiny spots of glue to the back of the piece and then lightly press it in place on your book.

Near right: Closed coils. *Left column, top to bottom:* peg, loose coil, eye-shaped coil, leaf shape. *Right column, top to bottom:* teardrop, petal, triangle, half-moon, tulip.

Far right: Open coils. *Top to bottom:* loose open coil, s-shaped scroll, full scroll, v-scroll, heart scroll.

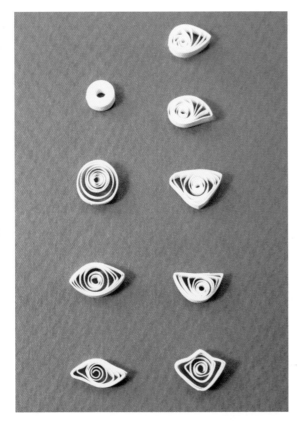

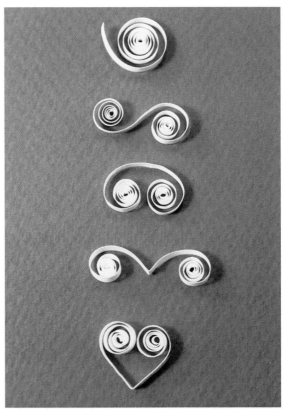

WEAVING

You can make an intricate yet sophisticated scrapbook cover by cutting decorative cover-weight paper into strips and then weaving them together. The instructions that follow show you how to make a woven design for the cover of a hinged book, similar to that on Myrna Bendett's book, shown below right. Myrna created this striking design by using a simple "over/under" tabby weave design with strips of paste papers. (Techniques for making paste papers will be discussed in Chapter 5.) The weaving was then glued in place over a front cover already wrapped in book cloth.

WHAT YOU'LL NEED

- *Weaving papers.* Any paper can be used, although light- to medium-weight paper will provide the smoothest turnovers when wrapping your weaving around a book cover. Choose two papers with coordinating colors, patterns, and/or textures; you may want to refer back to the "Working with Color" section on page 56. Tight paste-paper designs woven into loose suminagashi patterns or detailed patterned papers woven into solid-colored ones both make attractive designs. Even just varying the textures of solid-colored papers can make a stunning pattern.
- *Book cover.* You'll need a hard book cover that has already been wrapped in book cloth.

BASIC TECHNIQUE

Choose a sheet of paper 1¹/₂ inches (3.8 cm) longer and wider than your book cover and cut long parallel strips into it, leaving a 1-inch (2.5-cm) uncut margin at both the top and bottom of the sheet. In weaving, these vertical strips of paper are known as the *warp.* The uncut margins will function like a weaving frame to help hold your warp together as you weave in the loose, horizontal strips, called the *weft.*

Weft strips should be 2 inches (5 cm) longer than the warp. To cut strips with a straight edge, like those in Myrna's design, use a paper cutter or an X-acto knife and metal rule. For a more casual look, use edging scissors. The weft can also be made from thin strips of handmade paper or can be given artificial deckle edges.

Begin weaving by passing a weft strip over and under the bottom of the warp, letting the ends extend on either side. Weave a second weft strip by going under and then over the warp. Continue alternating in this way with every other weft strip, pushing each strip down as you go. When the warp is completely filled in, trim the top so that only a ¹/₂-inch (1.3-cm) margin remains to hold the weaving together.

To apply the weaving to your front cover (which should have already been wrapped in book cloth), spread a light coating of glue or lay a strip of double-sided adhesive on the top margin of your weaving and center the design, sticky-side down, on your book cover, with the weaving's top margin lined up parallel to the hinge groove. Adjust the weaving to make sure that the warp strips all lie flat against the book cover, and press the margin in place. Smooth the weaving down toward the fore edge of the book, using a thin coating of glue to help stabilize it if necessary. (But beware: too much glue will seep between the woven strips.) Cut off the bottom margin, which now lies along the fore edge of the cover, a little at a time as you fold over, trim, and glue the end of each warp strip over the cover's fore edge.

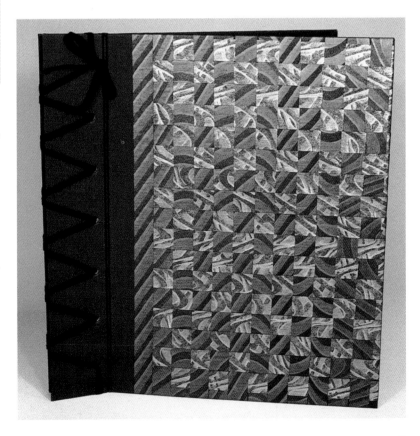

Myrna Bendett wove strips of paste paper in a tabby design to create this striking scrapbook cover. The book measures 8¹/₂ × 9 inches (21.6 × 23 cm), with ¹/₂-inch-wide (1.3-cm-wide) woven strips.

Next, fold over, trim, and glue the ends of each weft strip at the head and the tail of the book. Try to make the ends line up so they form smooth rows when the endpapers are applied over them.

As long as the warp strips remain attached to a margin of paper, weft strips can be easily woven through them to decorate a book cover. In this design, the weft strips run vertically.

Adhere a narrow strip of a coordinating decorative paper over the weaving margin at the spine of the book to cover the ends of the warp slits, folding it over the head and tail onto the inside cover. Finally, apply paper to line the inside cover. Repeat the entire process to create a woven back cover, if desired. (Then continue making and binding your book as described elsewhere for whatever style you have chosen.)

There are many variations to the above process. Small paper weavings with or without intact margin "frames" can be glued in place to decorate book covers or pages. And warp slits can even be cut directly into pages, with weft strips of paper, ribbon, or threads woven through them. One friend who keeps a journal of ethnic restaurants weaves fortune cookie sayings right into the book's pages!

PRESSED LEAVES AND FLOWERS

Depending on how fragile they are, leaves and flowers can be pressed and dried and then added to book pages or showcased on a cover. If their longevity is dubious, you may want to enclose them in glassine pockets or Mylar envelopes.

If it's not important that you use the exact leaf or flower you collected on your trip or saved from your bouquet, consider purchasing dried leaves and flowers that have been pressed professionally. They will have vivid colors and can be easily glued flat on your pages by carefully brushing white glue on them and pressing them in place. Carole Jackman, whose company Nature's Pressed carries a wide range of pressed flowers and foliage, suggests further protecting the flowers by coating them with a thinned white glue that remains flexible and dries clear (thus safeguarding them from those who will touch the flowers to see if they're real!).

Spring and summer flowers can provide beautiful accents for wedding, anniversary, or photo albums, while fall leaves on a scrapbook page can evoke memories of football games played on crisp autumn days. A hiker's journal, too, can be enhanced by wildflowers, like those found on the trail. Some of the more flexible dried leaves can also be coated with ink and used for leaf printing, and of course both leaves and flowers can be used in your papermaking.

A scrapbook page decorated with pressed leaves, created by Carole Jackman.

PIERCED METAL

Book artist Lea Everse has discovered yet another technique for creating book cover art: metal piercing. She discovered it by chance one day when, while embossing a sheet of copper foil, she accidentally punctured the foil. It became one of those happy accidents, and was developed into the following technique.

WHAT YOU'LL NEED

- Real copper foil, such as Foil Mirror Cardstock from New York Central Art Supply
- Rubber stamps
- Needles and parchment craft tools for piercing metal
- Pigment inks or acrylic paints for coloring metal
- Foam core, corrugated board, or thick felt

BASIC TECHNIQUE

Although some metal foil can be heated to create variegated coloring, Lea likes to add color by sponging it with pigment inks or acrylic paints. She then applies self-adhesive paper to the reverse side of the foil and stamps the image to be pierced on the paper. (You can also stamp the image directly on the bare metal with permanent ink, but the paper gives the design more stability and keeps it from rubbing off as you work.)

Lea places the metal foil facedown on a piece of foam core (or several sheets of corrugated board or thick felt), and then uses weaving and tapestry needles and parchment craft tools to pierce the foil, following the outline of the stamped image. To provide handles for the needles, she uses "pin vises," available at any hardware store. Alternatively, you can drill some wooden knobs and glue the heads of needles into them to form awls.

To make this cover art, Lea Everse stamped a design by Renaissance Rubber on copper foil, then pierced the outline of the rubber-stamped image.

CHAPTER 5

CREATING DECORATIVE PAPERS

The simple surface design techniques covered in this chapter can be used to create beautiful sheets of decorative paper, which can then be used to wrap book boards for stunning scrapbook, journal, and album covers. Decorative papers can also be used as background sheets for photos or memorabilia and, if they're lightweight, as endpapers or flyleaves. If they're heavy enough, such papers can even be used as covers for soft-bound albums.

This rich batik paper by Hélène Métivier was created by alternating color washes and wax applications. After the last application of color was applied, the wax was ironed out of the sheet. (Techniques for batik will be discussed on page 84.)

PRINTING TECHNIQUES

Some very simple printing techniques, including plastic-wrap, salt, and leaf printing, can be used to yield complex designs for your soft covers. Because leaf printing can be done on any type of paper, as explained below, you can use it to make decorative papers for the interiors of your books as well.

PLASTIC-WRAP PRINTING

Plastic-wrap prints are best made on heavy watercolor paper, so they are ideal for making soft album covers. While the technique is simple, the results are very dramatic.

Plastic-wrap printing on heavy watercolor paper was used to create the fractured design for this album cover. The stamped and thermal-embossed fish is by Fred Mullett.

Plastic wrap in place on the wet colors.

WHAT YOU'LL NEED

- *Colors.* Opaque calligraphy inks, drawing inks, or diluted acrylic paints can be used for color.
- *Paper.* Use a watercolor block or sheet of stretched watercolor paper. I like to use a watercolor block—a stack of paper that remains bound together until you pry a sheet free with a knife. The block will keep your paper stationary, which is useful as the drawing inks and acrylics you'll apply will make the paper wet enough to buckle if it's not held down while drying.
- *Water.* Use a spray bottle to add water.
- *Color applicators.* Pipettes should be used for squirting inks or a large watercolor mop brush for applying diluted acrylics.
- *Pearlescent pigments or metallic mica flakes.* Use these if you want to add some sparkle to your design.
- *Plastic wrap*
- *Thin vinyl gloves*

BASIC TECHNIQUE

Wearing the vinyl gloves, squirt or brush colors onto the surface of your paper until it is so wet that the colors form puddles. Add some mica or pearlescent pigments if desired. Use the spray bottle to add water and move the colors around, tilting your paper and the support it's on or using a very wet brush to coax them in a particular direction. Crumple a sheet of plastic wrap and place it over the wet colors, pressing down and manipulating the plastic to force the colors into designs. You can also squirt new colors under the plastic to further mix them.

While the colors are still wet, move the plastic around; pull it horizontally to create designs that look like rocky ledges—a perfect background for photos of the Grand Canyon—or scrunch it at random to create ice-like patterns for a scrapbook about an Alaskan holiday. When you are finished, place a book or board on top of the plastic until the colors have dried, then peel off the plastic to find a fragmented design just waiting to become a book cover.

SALT PRINTING

The same watercolor block and colors used for plastic-wrap printing can also be used for salt printing, which produces beautiful papers for soft-bound album covers.

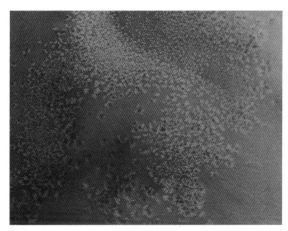

Designs like these are created when salt attracts the inks applied to heavy watercolor paper, forming the perfect cover for a dream journal.

WHAT YOU'LL NEED

- *Colors*. Opaque calligraphy inks, drawing inks, or diluted acrylic paints can be used for color.
- *Paper*. A watercolor block is recommended. You can also use sheets of stretched watercolor paper.
- *Color applicators*. Use a foam or mop brush to apply color.
- *Salt*. Experiment with different types of salt, such as table salt, kosher salt, and pretzel salt.
- *Thin vinyl gloves*

BASIC TECHNIQUE

Apply a liquid color wash to heavy watercolor paper with a foam or mop brush. While the paper is still very wet, sprinkle salt on it in either a random or controlled pattern. The salt will wick the color around it to produce mottled starburst patterns as it dries. Try using various types of salt for large and small starbursts. Let the color dry and then brush off the salt.

LEAF PRINTING

Leaf printing is a great way to decorate nature journals for remembering favorite hikes or scrapbook pages commemorating cross-country road trips, like the one made by artist Fred Mullett, shown on page 76. Leaf prints may be added to pages already bound in a book, or used to create decorative paper for use as a book cover.

WHAT YOU'LL NEED

- *Leaves*. Collect living leaves with textured surfaces and veins running through them. Ferns, ginkgos, and geraniums are especially good for doing allover patterns.
- *Plant press*. If you don't have a plant press, use a phone book weighted down with some heavy books to flatten the leaves and remove some of the moisture.
- *Sheet of Plexiglas*. This will provide a surface for inking leaves.
- *Colors*. Use water-based paints, ink pads, and/or brush markers for color.
- *Color applicators*. Watercolor brushes, brush markers, and/or raised stamp pads can be used to coat leaves with color.
- *Tweezers*

BASIC TECHNIQUE

Start by pressing your leaves in a purchased or makeshift plant press. Pressing time will vary; thinner leaves usually require about one hour. I've also had good results printing some leaves, especially ferns and tiny maple leaves, without pressing them at all. If you are using a raised stamp pad to color your leaves, the action of pressing the pad against the leaf may be all you need to render it flat.

If you're using brush markers or watercolor paints, coat the leaf as evenly as possible, creating color blends if you like. (If your leaf is coated with an oily residue, you may have to sponge it with a mild soap solution to remove the oils before printing.) If you're using a stamp pad, press the leaf against the pad if the leaf is small enough. (If it's a raised pad, press the pad against the leaf.) The prints by Fred Mullett, shown below, illustrate the different effects achieved by using watercolor paints and stamp pads.

Carefully lift the colored leaf and place it, ink-side down, on a journal page or sheet of paper. (If you have difficulty, use tweezers to lift the leaf.) Roll over the leaf with a soft printer's brayer, or place a piece of scrap paper over it and use your fingers to gently rub the back of the leaf, using constant pressure so as not to slide it around. When all parts of the leaf have made contact with the paper, carefully lift up the scrap paper and leaf. Protect the wet image until it's dry. Reapply color to the leaf and use it to print again, continuing until your design is complete.

These leaf prints by Fred Mullett show the different effects achieved by printing with a stamp pad (top) versus watercolor paints (bottom).

Using stamp pads and watercolor brush pens to create a sheet of decorative leaf-printed paper. The Color Box 2 Pigment Ink Option Pads pictured are made by Clearsnap, Inc. and work exceptionally well for leaf printing.

Fred Mullett used leaves collected on a cross-country trip to accent this combination scrapbook/sketchbook. He aptly describes the book as "a repository of memories, musings, and ideas."

ORIZOMEGAMI

A technique I often use for creating vivid papers to wrap hard book covers is called *orizomegami*, or fold-and-dye. Orizomegami involves accordion-pleating absorbent papers and then dipping the corners of the papers into cups of dye or squirting ink onto the folded bundle to create bright, kaleidoscopic designs.

WHAT YOU'LL NEED

- *Colors.* Drawing inks or Boku Undo marbling dyes should be used.
- *Paper.* Appropriate papers include thin absorbent rice papers, such as mulberry, sumi-e, or Loew-Cornell's Oriental Rice Paper.
- *Gloves or barrier hand cream*

BASIC TECHNIQUES

Fold your paper according to one of the diagrams on pages 78 and 79, pleating on the dotted lines to create different folds. Then dampen the folded bundle by dipping it in water and blotting with a towel. (I like to blot by placing several bundles side by side inside a hand towel and standing on it.)

Dip successive corners of the folded bundle into a shallow container full of color or use an applicator, such as a pipette or eyedropper, to apply color directly to the corners and folded edges. As the dye begins wicking into the paper, compress the bundle between your thumb and forefinger to force the dye deep into the center of the bundle or, alternatively, to stop the progression of the dye and force it back out. Clothespins can also be used to create resists that will prevent colors from saturating the entire paper. (They also provide convenient handles to protect your hands from the dye.) The contrast between these resist-preserved areas, which remain white or only lightly shaded, and the dye-colored sections, gives orizomegami papers the luminescence of stained glass.

When you've completed dyeing the bundle, carefully open it over scrap paper and leave it to dry, later flattening dried papers with an iron. If you're not happy with your design, simply refold

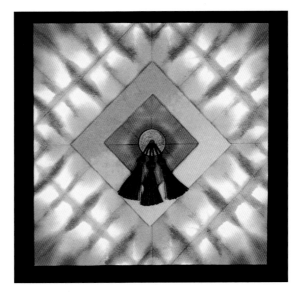

Orizomegami techniques were used to create the cover for this accordion-fold book, which is filled with lyrics from some of my favorite songs from the 1960s.

Dipping a folded bundle of paper into a container of dye.

the sheet in another configuration and dye it again. You can also use brush pens to add extra detail.

Orizomegami papers can be used as flyleaves, text page decoration, or cover papers. Because some papers are thin and absorbent, I prefer to use a dry adhesive film when using them to wrap book covers. If you place your book board on a sheet of adhesive film and carefully cut around the board with an X-acto knife, you can simply peel off the attached release sheet and flip the board over onto the decorated orizomegami paper. Then invert the board, burnish the paper down, miter the corners, and apply a minimum of glue to turn over and secure the flaps. Also, because some of the thin white rice papers can remain translucent even after dyeing, try to use book board or smooth mat board with a white covering rather than a gray one that might show through.

ORIZOMEGAMI

SQUARE OR RECTANGULAR FOLD

Accordion-pleat the paper vertically, then fold the resulting strip in a series of square or rectangular accordion folds.

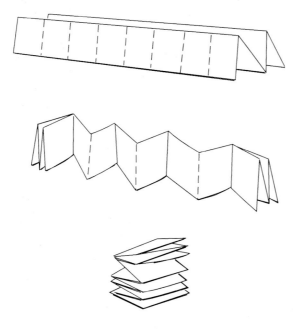

A pattern produced with the square or rectangular fold.

NARROW RECTANGULAR FOLD

Make ¹/₂-inch (1.3-cm) vertical pleats, then fold the resulting strip in long sections.

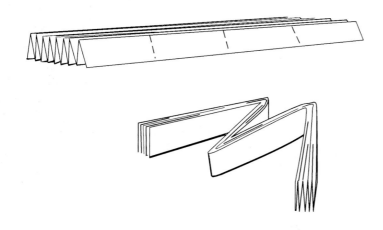

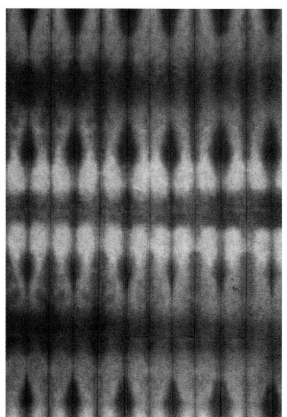

A pattern produced with the narrow rectangular fold.

TRIANGULAR FOLD

Accordion-pleat the paper vertically, then fold the resulting strip in a series of triangular accordion folds.

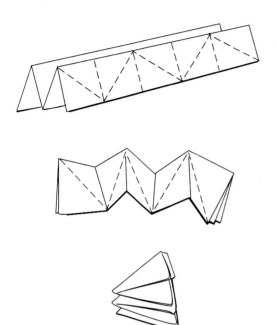

A pattern produced with the triangular fold.

PLEATED TRIANGLE FOLD

Fold a square paper in half lengthwise (A), then fold it in half again (B). Bring the bottom left corner up to meet the top right corner, forming a triangle (C). Fold the triangle into narrow pleats (D). Picture E shows a side view of the folded paper.

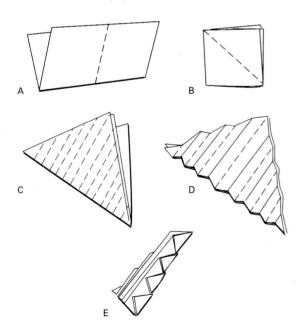

A pattern produced with the pleated triangular fold.

SUMINAGASHI MARBLING

Suminagashi marbling, the oldest and simplest type of marbling, is done by floating rings of Boku Undo dyes on water, blowing or fanning the rings into meandering or jagged lines, and then applying an absorbent paper to the floating colors to make a contact print. Like orizomegami papers, the delicate suminagashi designs make excellent endpapers, flyleaves, wrappings for hard covers, or even soft covers (depending on the thickness of your paper). When done on heavy handmade paper or commercial paper, like Mohawk Superfine, they can also be used as interior text pages for scrapbooks, albums, and journals.

Suminagashi is not the only type of marbling—oil color and watercolor marbling are also perfect for producing papers for the covers and pages of your books. These techniques remain outside the scope of this book, but complete instructions for all types of marbling can be found in my book *The Ultimate Marbling Handbook* (Watson-Guptill Publications, 1999).

BASIC TECHNIQUE

Place 1 teaspoon (5 ml) of two different Boku Undo colors into separate sections of your divided color container, and 1 teaspoon (5 ml) of water into a third. Add one drop of Photo-Flo to each color and to the water, stirring each well. Fill your marbling tray with water to a depth of about $1^1/2$ inches (3.8 cm) and skim off any dust that

WHAT YOU'LL NEED

- *Marbling tray.* For your first attempts, a photo tray or kitty litter pan can serve as a marbling tray. Later you may want to buy a professional tray with a separate rinse and skim section, which makes it easier to rinse marbled papers and skim off excess ink from the water in your tray. A baking pan can also be a workable alternative, although some have a coating that makes color sink.
- *Rinse board and bucket.* A purchased marbling tray will include a rinse board. If you're using a makeshift tray, you'll need a cookie sheet and a nearby sink or bucket for rinsing papers.
- *Water jug.* This will be used for dispensing water to rinse papers.
- *Drying rack or lines.* You'll need a support for your papers as they dry. An ideal drying support is clothesline strung with PVC pipe
- *Mixing tray.* You'll need a small plastic watercolor mixing tray with divided sections to hold the dyes. You can also use an ice cube tray.
- *Eyedroppers.* These will be used to transfer colors and dispersant.
- *Color applicators.* You'll need at least three inexpensive bamboo brushes for applying color. Get brushes that taper to a point, like Series BB by Loew-Cornell, no. 3 or 4.

- *Small plastic brush rest (optional)*
- *Paper towels.* Paper towels are helpful for drawing excess water out of your brushes.
- *Newspaper.* Newspaper should be cut into 2-inch-wide (5-cm-wide) strips for skimming the water in your marbling tray.
- *Colors.* Start off by using Boku Undo marbling dyes. Once you've had some marbling experience, you may want to experiment with Japanese ink sticks or cake colors to produce your own Japanese inks. You can also try using pigmented drawing inks straight from the bottle.
- *Kodak Photo-Flo 200.* This photographic chemical (a substitute for the pine resin traditionally used in Japan) helps disperse the Boku Undo colors, enabling them to spread and float on water. When added to a teaspoon of water, Photo-Flo creates a clear liquid used to preserve open areas between rings of floating colors.
- *Paper.* Paper used for marbling should be absorbent, such as kozo, Moriki, and Okawara, as well as many handmade and block print papers and Loew-Cornell's Oriental Rice Paper. Other papers with a high cotton content may also work. Experiment.
- *Gloves or barrier hand cream*

may have settled on the water by dragging a newspaper strip down the length of the tray, as shown at right (top).

Using a different brush for each color, stir the colors again. Gently touch the surface of the water in the center of the tray with the tip of one color-filled brush, releasing a circle of color. Now touch the center of this circle with the tip of the Photo-Flo brush; the color should react by spreading out into a ring. Continue to alternately apply color (either of your two colors) and clear solution until a number of concentric rings are formed, as shown at right (middle).

When you have finished creating rings, gently blow them into a design. Form meandering lines of color by blowing gently from the side of the tray; to form jagged lines, blow sharply from above or wave a handheld fan, as shown on page 82. If you marble with very little water in your tray, you can create unusual designs by dragging a single hair through the color rings. Alternatively, try a special tool I've devised that works more easily to produce the same image: a cat whisker (volunteered by my cat, Camille) taped to the wrong end of a bamboo brush.

After patterning your colors, slowly lay a sheet of absorbent paper onto the floating image, as shown in the illustration on page 82, being careful not to flop the paper down and disturb the design. (If you're working with paper that's very fragile, leave 1 inch [2.5 cm] of the edge of the paper dry to help you pick it up.) As soon as the paper has absorbed the colors, pick up the edge farthest from you and peel the paper up off the water onto your rinse board or cookie sheet. If you see any colors bleeding off the paper, gently pour water over it to rinse (also shown on page 82). Then drape the sheet over your drying rack or clothesline. When the paper is dry, place it under a board to flatten it or iron it on the unmarbled side.

To create a double-image "ghost print," my favorite for book cover design, try marbling a dry sheet a second time. The intersecting lines will create new patterns and colors to produce fascinating images.

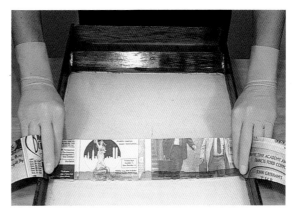

Skimming the water-filled marbling tray before applying the color.

Applying color and clear solution to build up a number of concentric color rings.

If you are working a design with two colors, you can learn to deposit colors more quickly by holding two color-filled brushes in one hand and the dispersant brush in the other.

Fanning the inks to create a pattern of jagged lines.

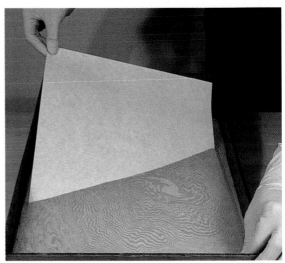

Laying a sheet of absorbent paper onto the floating colors.

Rinsing the printed paper to remove any excess color.

The foreign currency was so beautiful!

A page from a travel scrapbook, with double-image suminagashi marbling on the background paper.

CHALK MARBLING

This technique is a kind of faux marbling—very simple to do, but quite effective for producing colorful papers that can be used to wrap hard covers or accent interior pages. Chalk-marbled papers can be laminated to mat board to create shaped books, like the one made by Delia Quinn shown at right. They can also be layered in progressively smaller sheets, each providing a border for the next, to decorate book covers and pages.

WHAT YOU'LL NEED

- *Chalk.* You'll need chalk in several colors. Make sure it is not the dust-free variety.
- *A dull kitchen knife*
- *Paper.* Use medium-weight drawing paper.
- *Newspaper.* Cut the newspaper into 2-inch-wide (5-cm-wide) strips for skimming, as in suminagashi marbling.
- *Acrylic spray fixative*

BASIC TECHNIQUE

Use the dull kitchen knife to lightly scrape the sides of differently colored pieces of chalk over a pan of water. The multicolored chalk dust will float on the surface of the water. Lay a sheet of paper on the floating dust, as in suminagashi marbling, to make a contact print. Hang the wet paper or lay it flat to dry. When the paper has dried, treat it like a pastel drawing and spray it lightly with fixative to keep it from . . . chalking.

Before making another print, skim the water in your pan with a newspaper strip to remove any chalk residue (see illustration on page 81).

A chalk-marbled book cover by Delia Quinn.

BATIK

atik or wax-resist papers are easy to make and can be used to create a background paper for a photo, as shown below, or to produce an exotic-looking book cover. Although batik is usually done on text-weight drawing paper using watercolor paints or dyes, you can also experiment with other materials. Hélène Métivier, for example, produces stunning batik papers by painting sturdy rice papers with fabric dyes and wax.

The principle behind the batik process is the same for fabric or paper. When wax is applied to a material it forms a waterproof barrier that repels any liquid color applied over it. If you drip spots of wax on a white sheet of paper, for instance, and then coat the paper with a wash of yellow dye, you'll

wind up with a yellow sheet of paper with white spots. If you then apply a second layer of wax using random brush strokes, followed by a wash of green dye, you'll end up with a multicolored sheet. The paper will be green, with white spots still protected by the first waxing, and yellow brushstrokes where the second waxing maintained the yellow dye. Note that each color you apply will blend with the previous color on any unprotected areas, so choose your color scheme carefully, and work from light to dark.

This page from Hélène Métivier's scrapbook of feline photos shows how well a batik paper can function as a photo border.

WHAT YOU'LL NEED

- *Wax.* Begin with a mixture of paraffin and beeswax or batik wax, available in art supply stores.
- *A double boiler.* This is the safest way to melt wax.
- *Wax applicators.* Large and small disposable watercolor brushes should be used for brushing and splattering the wax.
- *Paper.* Most types of paper can be used, as long as they can withstand being wet with liquid colors. Some of the softer papers may retain more of the wax, but this shouldn't pose a problem.
- *Colors.* Inexpensive watercolors can be used.
- *Color applicators.* Wide bamboo brushes, poly foam brushes, and mop brushes can be used to apply a good wash of color. I recommend Loew-Cornell's 1-inch (2.5-cm) oval mop brush.
- *Newspapers.* You'll need lots of newspapers to protect tabletops from wax and color and to absorb wax as it's ironed out of papers.
- *An iron.* An iron is needed to remove the wax from papers after you've applied your last coat of dye. Use one without steam vents, if possible, as wax can block the vents.

BASIC TECHNIQUE

Although fine tools can be used to make very structured batik designs, it's great fun to make abstract designs by simply brushing, splashing, and splattering the wax. If you've been very precise in making your albums and journals it will feel especially good to let go and make some avant-garde batik papers.

First, melt some wax in a double boiler, being careful not to let it overheat. The wax must be carefully monitored as it can give off noxious smoke or even ignite if it gets too hot. When the wax has melted, dip a brush into it and begin making designs on a sheet of light-colored paper. The wax will begin to dry almost immediately, so you must work quickly. (Because of this, some artists prefer to work out their designs beforehand.)

Once the wax has dried, apply a watercolor wash using a light-value color (such as yellow) over the entire sheet of paper. Let the color dry, then brush, drip, or splatter on more wax, followed by another wash of a darker, harmonious color. Continue to build up layers of wax and color, bearing in mind that each coat of wax will maintain the last color applied.

When the final coat of color has dried, unveil your masterpiece by removing the wax from the sheet. Sandwich the paper batik between several layers of newspaper and press it with a warm iron, changing the newspaper until all the wax has been ironed out of the sheet.

Brushing a layer of wax onto a batik paper in progress.

A batik paper created by Hélène Métivier.

STENCILING

By applying color through an opening cut in heavy paper, acetate, or a brass plate, you can create stenciled designs to use as book covers, as background papers for photographs, or as accents to help convey the theme of a journal or scrapbook. Lynell Harlow, whose meticulous work is shown below, produces a line of brass stenciling and embossing plates that make stenciling very easy. Although I usually advocate creating your own stencils from scratch, hers are just too hard to resist. Because you can combine images using several of her brass plates, thereby creating your own unique designs, purists can take heart that this isn't really cheating, but just eliminating an intermediate step in the design process!

If you still want to start from scratch, purchase translucent stencil acetate and trace or draw designs on it, using an X-acto knife to cut your stencils. Remember that a stencil should represent a *negative* of the design: when you apply color through the holes of the stencil, the *positive* will be left on your paper. Precut stencils can be a valuable aid to see how the bridge—the solid piece of acetate that separates parts of a design—helps to accent and define the silhouette. Precut acetate stencils can also be altered with an X-acto knife to make them more your own.

Lynell Harlow repeated a stenciled design to compose an allover pattern, creating this stunning page for her photo album.

WHAT YOU'LL NEED

- *Stencils.* Stencils can be made from heavy paper, acetate, or brass plates.
- *Color applicators.* Stencil brushes with natural bristles cut to the same length can be used to apply colors. For small, detailed areas, it's handy to have small color applicators. To begin with, three brushes, ¹/₄ to 1 inch (0.6 to 2.5 cm) in diameter, will be adequate.
- *Paper towels.* These are used to remove excess color from your brushes and stencils.
- *Paper.* Just about any text- or cover-weight paper that's not too absorbent can be stenciled.
- *Colors.* Use stencil paints with a creamy, rather than runny, consistency. Paint sticks, which are basically paint in solid form (available at art and craft supply stores), work well and eliminate the bleeding under stencils that sometimes occurs with liquid colors.

BASIC TECHNIQUE

Begin by taping your cut stencil in position over your paper. (A brass stencil can sometimes be simply held in place.) To charge your brush with color, hold it perpendicular and just touch the surface of the color container with the flat edge of the applicator. Then, still holding your brush perpendicular, tap it against a paper towel or piece of scrap paper to distribute the color evenly. The brush should be almost dry when it's used; this keeps the color from bleeding under the stencil openings and blurring the edges of your designs. If you're using a paint stick, deposit a layer of color on waxed paper before picking it up with your brush.

Two methods of applying stencil paint include stippling, or tapping the perpendicular brush on the stencil opening until it has been covered with color, and rouging, which is done by moving an almost dry brush in a circular motion to rub paint into the stencil openings. Work on top of the acetate or brass plate at first, moving from the edge of the opening to its center to lay down a thin layer of color.

It's not necessary to fill in the entire stencil opening with intense color. Sometimes a darker shading on the edges of the opening, leading to a lighter concentration of color in the center of a design, as shown in the floral stencil by Lynell Harlow (opposite), can be very effective.

When you've finished applying color through your stencil, remove the tape and pick the pattern straight up so as not to smudge the stenciled design. Be sure to wipe off any color on the stencil before it dries. If you're doing repeat patterns to be used as background papers for album pages or book covers, make sure that the stencil is totally clean before moving it to another position on your paper. Put your finished paper in a safe place to dry. If stenciling a bound journal page, carefully prop the book open; oil stenciled pieces sometimes need several hours to dry.

Applying a thin layer of paint with a stencil brush.

SPRAYING, SPATTERING, AND

Spraying, spattering, and sponging techniques, commonly used to create background designs in card making, can also be used to decorate papers for bookmaking. You can spatter, sponge, or spray through a stencil you've cut or made, or through any object with openings, such as plastic rug backings, doilies, radiator screens, and so on.

WHAT YOU'LL NEED

- *Colors*. Acrylic paint (either in spray form or thinned with water), drawing inks, and stamp pads can all be used for various techniques.
- *Color applicators*. Anything from ordinary sponges to vegetable brushes and toothbrushes can be used to apply color. For neater and more consistently sized spatters, try using the Speckling Brush made by Loew-Cornell. When you coat the brush tips with paint and then turn a handle to rotate the brush against a metal pin, the paint spatters in the direction in which you turn the handle.
- *Stencils*. Any object with openings can be used, from precut stencils to found objects.

BASIC TECHNIQUES

To spray a design, use acrylic spray paint and apply color sparingly through a stencil. Hold the can of paint about 18 inches (46 cm) from the stencil, propping the stencil and paper up vertically and then quickly laying them flat after spraying to avoid drips. Practice spraying in short bursts, keeping the can moving as you work. You can also scatter objects like leaves, plastic photographic slide mounts, metal washers, wood, or heavy paper cut-outs on your paper and then spray around them. Spray with one color, let the paint dry, then move the objects to another position and spray again. Shades of the same color or different colors can be used.

To spatter a design, use acrylic paint thinned with water or drawing inks. Simply place some paint or ink in a flat dish, coat a toothbrush or vegetable brush with color, and then tap off some of the paint. With the brush bristles facing up and the front of the brush tipped downward, draw a tongue depressor toward you over the bristles, spattering paint on your paper. If you're working inside, spatter inside a cardboard box to avoid decorating your walls and floor, too.

Janet Hofacker used spray webbing to enhance this album page. Columns were created with a rubber stamp made by Stamp Francisco.

SPONGING

If used judiciously, spray webbing, available in most craft stores, can also be used effectively to decorate a photo album page, like the one shown by Janet Hofacker opposite. Begin by spraying the webbing off the paper, then use a sweeping motion to draw the can over the paper. The webbing should fall onto the paper as you pass over it.

To apply a fine mist of color to your book pages, use an airbrush or a blitzer—a less expensive version of the airbrush. By squeezing the bulb of the blitzer, air is forced into the tip of a color marker, releasing a mist of color. Claudia Lee uses another technique to achieve similar results: she mixes papermaking pigments with water, puts them in a spray bottle, and then applies them through a grid to create stenciled designs.

Sponges can also be used to create designs. Use different types of sponges, from cosmetic sponges to sea sponges to sponges with large and small openings, and tap them against stamp pads or dip them in acrylic paints to load them with color. You can also try cutting off a sponge's hard edges for rounded corners that will produce softer designs. Before you begin sponging, blot

Above: Claudia Lee created this paper by spattering dyes through a rug backing. More consistent (but perhaps less arty) designs can be made by using the spatter brush shown.

Left: This book by Janet Hofacker features a sponged design on its cover.

some of the color off on a paper towel. Then apply color through openings in a stencil or sponge at random over a previously decorated sheet to add more texture. Try creating different effects by varying the color or amount of paint in the sponge. A whisper of gold or silver paint sponged over a handmade paper can enliven the border around a black-and-white photograph without overpowering the image. For more vivid designs, sponge with one color, let dry, and then continue with another. Making successive sponge prints will create interesting color blends and produce papers for both the interiors and exteriors of books.

If you sponge with a minimum of paint and go beyond the border of your stencil to highlight its silhouette as well as its interior openings, an enhanced design like the romantic doily-stenciled image by Gail Crosman Moore (shown below) will result. Paper masks may also be used to create interesting border designs that you can accent with sponging or spraying. You can also try tearing paper in exaggerated hill and valley shapes, placing them in patterns on your page, and then sponging, spattering, or spraying over them in different colors to create mountainous forms for a nature journal or book of travel narratives.

Paint can be sprayed or sponged beyond the border of a stencil to highlight its silhouette as well as its interior openings. The books shown here are by Gail Crosman Moore.

DRY EMBOSSING

Embossing creates a raised or recessed surface in a sheet of paper, giving it a decorative pattern or textured surface. It is particularly effective on white paper as the play of light and shadow gives the raised design a certain elegance. Other types of embossing—wet embossing and thermal embossing—will be explained on pages 108 and 98, respectively.

WHAT YOU'LL NEED

- *Embossing patterns.* The brass plates used for stenciling can also be used to create raised designs on scrapbook and photo album pages. Found objects like the decorative metal screens used to cover radiators and the shapes that appear in plastic drafting templates can also be used.
- *Paper.* Art papers, handmade papers, and the cover- and text-weight papers used on your hand-made (or purchased) books can all be embossed.
- *Ball-tipped burnisher.* A ball-tipped burnisher, available at any craft supply shop, will allow you to reproduce detailed designs, such as ornate borders, that are perfect for framing photos and memorabilia. A stylus can also be used.

Dry-embossed designs make great raised frames for photos, as on this album page decorated with sumina-gashi-marbled paper.

TIP

If your paper has a tooth, like Canson Mi-Teintes and many other art papers, you may find that the embossing tool tends to drag as you move it across the paper. To remedy the situation, rub the burnisher on a piece of waxed paper to help it glide more easily.

BASIC TECHNIQUE

To use a brass stencil for embossing, place it on the front of the paper you wish to emboss, securing it with a small piece of removable tape. Invert the paper and stencil and place them stencil-side down over a light box or against a sunny window. Working on the back of the paper, use a stylus, ball-tipped burnisher, or other blunt tool to press the paper into the illuminated opening. Move the burnisher around the edge of the cut-out until a crisp pattern appears, turning the stencil and attached paper as you work to reach all parts of the design. Make sure the paper remains attached to the stencil until the image is completely embossed as it's practically impossible to get the stencil back in position once it's been moved. If you wish to add color to your design, leave the stencil in place and use a small stenciling brush to add color to the work.

Using a ball-tipped burnisher and brass stencil to emboss a design for a scrapbook page.

PASTE PAPERS

aste-paper designs have been used for centuries to decorate book covers and endpapers. The techniques are simple and will enable you to make a wide range of graphic and colorful designs to cover your handmade scrapbooks, albums, and journals. The basic method involves dampening a sheet of paper, coating it with colored paste, and then drawing various implements through the paste to create patterns. Kitchen tools, hairpicks, chopsticks, and lots of found objects can be used to make deceptively sophisticated designs. By adding graining combs and calligraphy pens to your store of patterning tools, your design options will be greatly increased.

WHAT YOU'LL NEED

- *Saucepan.* You'll need a 2-quart (1.9-l) saucepan to cook the paste.
- *Measuring cup.* This will be used to measure ingredients for making the paste.
- *Teaspoons.* Use old teaspoons to stir paint into the prepared paste.
- *Sponges.* Sponges will be used to wet the paper, to make sponge prints in paste (if desired), and for cleanup.
- *Gloves (optional)*
- *Small plastic water bucket.* This gives you a place to dip the sponge for cleanup and for sponging down the paper to be pasted.
- *Large fine-mesh strainer.* Use this to strain the paste.
- *Brushes.* Several large 2- to 4-inch (5- to 10-cm) high-quality house-painting brushes are needed, one for each color. Don't purchase inexpensive ones as they will quickly lose their bristles (usually in the middle of making a design!).
- *Colored paste containers.* Plastic food storage containers with snap-tight lids are ideal. They must be big enough to accommodate your paint brush.
- *Work surface.* A piece of Plexiglas 3 inches (7.6 cm) larger on all sides than the paper you plan to pattern provides a good work surface. Alternatives include an old Formica or enamel tabletop.
- *Large plastic storage box.* A large plastic tub filled with water will be perfect for wetting your papers.
- *Patterning tools.* Plastic hairpicks and forks, buttons, rubber stamps, and chopsticks are but a few of the many patterning tools you may already have on hand. Other great implements for making designs include metal and rubber graining combs, crumpled pieces of newspaper, multiple-line calligraphy pens, and potter's tools. Even corks, pieces of cardboard, and plastic milk cartons can be fashioned into paste-paper stamps and combs with assistance from an X-acto knife or some scissors. Rubber brayers carved with a mat knife can also yield interesting designs.
- *Paper.* Most nonabsorbent medium-weight papers are fine for making paste paper designs. You won't be able to use soft Japanese papers as the paper must be strong enough to withstand having tools drawn across it in a dampened state without shredding. I use Canson Mi-Teintes, Strathmore, and Mohawk Superfine papers, but many offset printing papers also work fine. Just be sure not to get a paper that's too thick for the bookbinding project you plan to use it on.
- *Paints.* A good brand of acrylic paint, like Golden or Liquitex, gives excellent results. (Don't buy the fluid acrylics as they tend to dilute the paste too much.) Invest in a range of colors and be sure to include some metallics and pearlescent colors. You can also add Pearlex or mica powders to your acrylics to make them sparkle (which looks particularly dramatic on black charcoal paper).
- *Paste.* Rice flour, wheat flour, cornstarch, and methyl cellulose can all be used to make paste (or starch) papers. Glycerine (available at pharmacies) and dish detergent are also added to some paste formulas.

Paste-paper designs can vary greatly, depending upon the type of tool used to create them. Various combs, a chopstick, carved rubber brayers, and a wadded-up piece of newspaper were used to create the papers shown.

MAKING THE PASTE

Many paste-paper makers swear by a favorite recipe for their paste; the following are the recipes I use when making papers for covering albums and scrapbooks. Note that the flour recipe produces papers with a more granular texture, while papers covered and patterned with the starch and methyl cellulose pastes tend to be smoother. I usually opt for the starch recipe as it seems to hold patterned images a bit better.

Flour Paste: Measure 3 cups (710 ml) water and set aside. Blend 4 tablespoons (60 g) rice flour and 3 tablespoons (45 g) wheat flour in a saucepan with a little of the water. Add the remaining water and cook the mixture over medium heat, stirring constantly, until it resembles a thin custard. Remove the paste from the heat and stir in $1/2$ teaspoon (2.5 ml) glycerin and 1 teaspoon (5 ml) dish detergent to keep the paste smooth and pliable. Let the paste cool and thicken before pushing it through a strainer to remove any lumps.

Cornstarch Paste: Mix $1/4$ cup (60 ml) cornstarch with $1/4$ cup (60 ml) water until well blended. Then add 1 cup (240 ml) water and heat the mixture while stirring until it resembles a thick custard. Finally stir in $1/2$ cup (120 ml) water to thin it down. Let the mixture cool and thicken before pushing it through a strainer to remove any lumps.

Methyl Cellulose Paste: Mix the paste according to package directions, which may vary among manufacturers. You want the paste to be about the consistency of toothpaste when you brush it onto the papers.

BASIC TECHNIQUE

The instructions that follow have been divided into three stages: coloring the paste, applying the paste, and creating a pattern.

COLORING THE PASTE

Divide the paste among several bowls, putting about $1/2$ cup (120 ml) in each, and add about 2 to 3 teaspoons (10 to 15 ml) of color to the paste in

Using a sponge to remove excess water, press out air bubbles, and flatten the paper.

Brushing colored paste on the dampened paper.

Using a rubber graining comb to create scalloped designs on a paste-covered sheet.

each bowl. Add the paint gradually to achieve the desired color, bearing in mind that the colored paste will dry on the paper a bit lighter than it looks in the container. If you want to darken a color a bit, add just a touch of black, as it can easily overpower other colors. Add some metallics or pearlescents to your paints to make the papers shimmer.

APPLYING THE PASTE

Prepare your paper by relaxing it in a tray or sink of water. Just drag the paper through the water, wetting both sides, and then let it drip for a moment before carrying it to the Plexiglas and laying it flat. Apply pressure as you stroke the paper from the center outward with a damp sponge to remove excess water, pressing out any air bubbles and flattening it completely. If any wrinkles remain in the paper, your patterning will make them even more noticeable.

Load a large 2- to 4-inch (5- to 10-cm) paintbrush with paste and brush it evenly on your paper. Use horizontal strokes to cover the paper with a thin layer of paste, then go back over the paper with vertical strokes to assure a good color application. If you're using different colored pastes on the same sheet, brush in one direction only to avoid totally mixing the colors and making them muddy. Instead, try letting the colored pastes overlap slightly to make subtle color blends.

CREATING A PATTERN

Allover repeat patterns are particularly striking for book covers and are easy to make in paste. Explore them by making rows of diagonal or horizontal lines with a pick or comb and then crossing them at regular intervals with vertical lines. Use a calligraphy pen to make a wavy line next to a straight one, or place a thin line made with a chopstick next to a thick line made with a plastic spackle knife to add contrast. When using combs, try angling the combing tool slightly toward you as you draw it through the paste. This will help make your movements smoother and the designs more pronounced.

Vary the direction and type of movement you make to create straight lines, eccentric zigzags (good for a life journal), or long gentle curves or scallops that might suggest waves for a scrapbook about boating trips. It's easy to create designs that not only decorate paper for book covers but also relate to the theme of the book. If you're using a photo on the cover of your album, you can design a paste paper background to coordinate with the colors or repeat curves, lines, or dots that appear on clothing or in the background of the image.

You can also explore designs made by stamping a paste-covered paper with various objects. A crumpled piece of plastic wrap or newspaper, rubber stamps, and carved linoleum blocks can be used, as well as shapes cut from balsa wood and objects made of rubber, cork, metal, wood, and plastic. To get the best image, wipe off any residual paste clinging to the object before using it a second time. Two pasted sheets of paper can also be pressed together, face-to-face, and then pulled apart to create a textured print that resembles foliage. (When making this type of design, be careful not to create a buildup of paste that might dry and crack when the dried paper is wrapped around a piece of book board.)

To dry paste papers, avoid crimps by draping them over a rack or clothesline covered with PVC pipe. Flatten out dried papers by ironing them on their reverse sides. Be sure to use a wet sponge to wipe off any paste left on your work surface before beginning another sheet.

After a sheet has dried, you can rewet it and coat it with paste again to create a second image on top of the first. The colors and pattern of the primary image will peek through and can produce a sheet with great dimension. Combed papers can look especially brilliant when they're coated with gold or silver paste and patterned a second time. As redampened paste can be a bit fragile, however, it's best to use rubber and plastic tools when making combed multiple-image designs.

VARIATION: FAUX PASTE PAPERS

The combing techniques described above can also be used with acrylic paint alone to create highly textured papers. Although the designs will be too brittle for covering book boards or for use as soft covers, they can be used to accent covers and pages. Lea Everse, who jokes that she's too lazy to do real paste papers, uses this technique to create raised designs that resemble paste papers but have a lot more dimension. She usually starts with a small piece of glossy or coated paper and squeezes out thin lines of acrylic paint in a checkerboard or plaid pattern, laying her first line of paint right on the edge of the paper. Then she uses tools like those used for paste papers to create patterns in the paint.

A faux paste paper design by Lea Everse, with rubber stamp design by Stamp Out Cute.

RUBBER STAMPING

Rubber-stamped images can be used to accent scrapbook, album, and journal covers and pages or can be used in allover repeat patterns to create decorative papers for wrapping hard book covers. Because stamps can be applied to just about any surface, they can also be used on thick watercolor paper to make soft-bound books.

Although it's great to cut your own stamps from erasers, or to have personally designed stamps professionally cut, most book artists purchase premade stamps and use their creativity to blend colors, combine images, or create artfully raised designs with embossing powders. There are millions of rubber stamp designs available so you can easily find an image that relates to the theme of your book, whether it's Indonesian masks or mountain-bike trails.

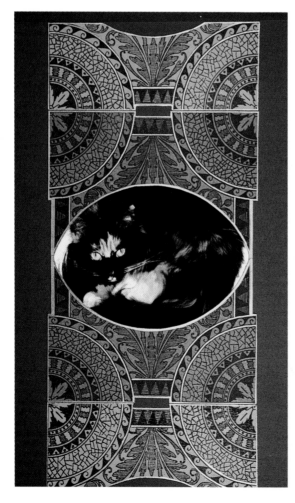

To create this scrapbook page, Hélène Métivier used linked stamp designs by Magenta Rubber Stamps.

WHAT YOU'LL NEED

- *Rubber stamp.* Purchased stamps, stamps you've created, or stamps you've had laser-cut from original designs can all be used.
- *Rubber stamp inks.* Raised stamp pads come in a range of solid, metallic, and rainbow colors. The rainbow pads include several bands of color, allowing you to do multicolored designs. Opaque pigment brush markers are also good inking tools. They come in a huge range of colors; buy the biggest set you can afford.

  Another great tool for applying color to rubber stamps is the watercolor brush pen, which allows you to blend colors on a stamp or ink parts of a stamp in different colors. Unfortunately, the stamp sometimes begins to dry before you use it—especially when you get interested in creating just the right shade of thalo blue, with just a touch more green to match another part of your scrapbook page. If this happens, exhale onto your stamp just before using it to remoisten the drying areas. (Pens with opaque pigment inks tend to dry more slowly, so you can use them at a more leisurely pace.)
- *Paper.* You can stamp on almost any paper, although the effects will vary. Some handmade and unsized papers stamped with water-based inks will create beautiful, soft-edged designs. If you're stamping on a completed cover or page that's already bound in a journal, try stamping on a scrap of the same paper first to see how you like the results.

BASIC TECHNIQUE

To use a stamp pad, merely press your stamp against it with enough force to deposit ink on the relief design. Be careful not to press too hard or you'll ink the background of the stamp. Raised stamp pads, which come in various formats for inking large or small stamps, are even easier to use. Just press the pad against the stamp to deposit ink. Colorbox Pigment Inkpads and Pigment Option Pads, both made by Clearsnap, Inc., are wonderful for inking stamps. They are made with archival quality, fade-resistant inks and come in various color combinations.

To begin stamping, press your inked stamp against your paper firmly, without rocking it. If you want to create images that fade in and out, re-ink the stamp about every third stamping. Rotate the stamp 90 or 180 degrees to create other variations in a repetitive design. If your stamp is mounted on a Lucite base, you will be able to see through the base to help position the stamp for repeat patterns.

Interesting border designs for album pages can be made by alternating stamp designs or by stamping in one color and then restamping over the initial image in a related color with a lighter value, allowing the images to overlap slightly. By using stamps with straight edges, like the triangles, wedges, and arrows produced by ERA Graphics, you can create interlocking designs to decorate borders or spill across book pages. These striking designs will link not only your stamped images, but also the photos and/or memorabilia on the page.

Try creating an attractive background page for photos or memorabilia by inking a stamp with several colors and using it to stamp a repeat design, beginning with part of the image off the paper's edge and then filling the entire page. The same technique can be used to create a patterned paper for a book cover. To create a sheet with lots of dimension, try stamping an allover repeat design with a pattern or texture stamp that resembles lace, granite, or grass. When the sheet is dry, go back and stamp over the entire sheet with another texture stamp, using a related color. If designs are simple, sometimes a third image can be added without the sheet becoming too busy.

When you're through using a stamp or decide to switch ink color, be sure to stamp off excess ink and then clean the stamp with a damp towel or sponge to prevent surprise color mixtures from cropping up and ruining designs. Commercial stamp cleaning pads may be necessary if you're using oil-based pigments.

TIP

To create stamped images that resemble those made with watercolor paints, ink your stamp with a water-based ink and then dampen it with a fine mist from a spray bottle before stamping.

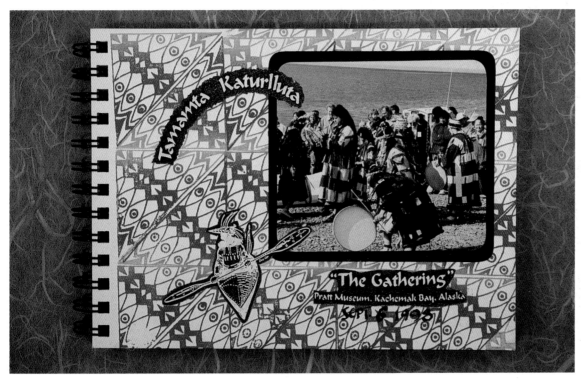

Roberta Altshuler stamped an allover repeat design to create this unique background paper for photos of her trip to Alaska.

VARIATION: THERMAL EMBOSSING

By applying embossing powder to a wet stamped image and then heating and melting the powder with a heat gun, you can create a raised glossy design similar to the commercial thermography designs seen on fine stationery and business cards. Embossing powders are available in many solid, metallic, and pearlescent colors. Interference colors that show up especially well on black paper can also be used, and clear embossing powder will highlight colors stamped beneath them to give the stamped image a glossy, wet look.

To emboss an image, first coat your stamp with a slow-drying ink; use clear ink if you plan to coat the image with a colored embossing powder. Stamp your image on the paper, then sprinkle the embossing powder over it while it is still wet. Tap the paper to spread the powder over the stamped image, then shake excess powder onto a piece of folded paper so that it can easily be returned to the bottle. Use a cotton swab or small brush to wipe away any powder that's clinging to parts of the paper you don't intend to emboss. Then heat the powder (from above, using an embossing gun) to melt it and create the embossed image, as shown at left. If desired, fill in the interior of an embossed image with brush markers. If you get color on the embossed surface, just use a cotton swab to wipe it off.

Fred B. Mullett, who creates striking stamps from nature prints, is a master of stamp embossing and coloring techniques. He often uses a spot application of differently colored embossing powders to selected areas of a stamped image, a process he describes as "like painting with plastic." The embossed fish shown on page 74 is one of Fred's designs.

Lea Everse, who also works magic with embossing powders and stamps, sometimes colors the paper before stamping her images. She began

Using a heat gun to thermal emboss a stamped design. The finished multicolored embossed fish by Fred Mullett has had accents added with a watercolor brush pen.

This book features one of Lea Everse's stamped and embossed designs on its cover. Lea mounted parts of the design on foam core to elevate them and give the work added dimension. (Stamp designs by Judikins.)

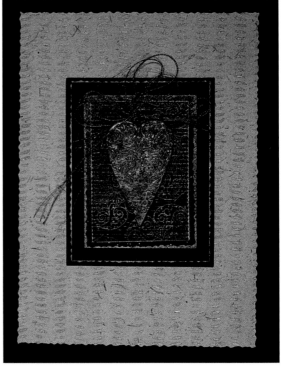

An example of Lea Everse's multilayered embossing. (Stamp design by Stamp Francisco.)

the stunning composition shown opposite (bottom left) by using Marvy Metallic felt-tip pens on glossy black cardstock. Lea first sprayed the cardstock with water and then covered the entire surface with different colored markers. When she tipped the card, the colors ran and swirled together. After the cardstock dried, she stamped and embossed it. Lea cut out the stamped leaves and squares and mounted them on foam core to elevate them from the background design and give the work added dimension.

Lea has also perfected a technique called "multilayered embossing," which looks like encaustic stamping (see opposite, bottom right). Instead of using wax, however, Lea substitutes embossing powder. She builds up several layers of melted powder on her paper and then uses a rubber stamp to deeply impress the image. She cautions that the technique works best with deeply etched, well-trimmed stamps with no background that could distort the impression.

Thermal-embossed images are usually not pliable enough to use on decorative paper for wrapping hard covers (unless you position them so they don't appear near a turnover). You can, however, stamp and emboss images on finished book covers or layer them with background papers, as Lea has so artfully done, to create stamp art that can be mounted on existing book covers.

VARIATION: PAINTING WITH STAMP PADS

Yet another variation on stamping has been perfected by Hélène Métivier, who creates stunning page and cover designs by using ColorBox Petal Point Pigment Option Pads and ColorBox 2 Option Plate Inkpads directly on colored paper. Hélène uses the ink pad to dab or brush ink onto cover-weight paper, as shown above right, letting one color show through or border the next. Light or metallic colors on dark paper are especially beautiful. Because the ColorBox inks dry very slowly, you can lay down many layers of color before any begin to dry. Try using the corner, side, or flat area of the ink pad to lightly rub or brush colors across the paper to build up a design. Hélène also suggests covering the entire design with clear embossing powder to give the whole image an enameled look.

Using ColorBox Petal Point Pigment Option Pads to begin a paper.

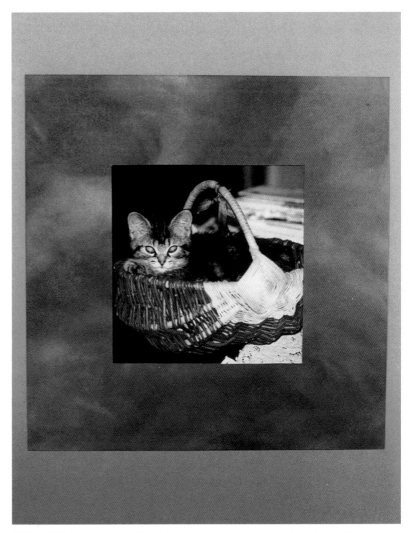

Hélène Métivier created this rich background paper by using direct pigment-to-paper techniques, which involve using raised ink pads to paint decorative designs on paper without using a rubber stamp.

RUBBINGS

Rubbing, or frottage, is the same technique used in grade school to reproduce the image of a penny onto a piece of paper. You simply hold a piece of paper over a textured surface and rub it with a crayon to transfer the design to the paper. Many people have done brass rubbings in medieval churches, or tombstone rubbings in old cemeteries. But quite ordinary, flat objects like screens, doormats, chair seats, and even manhole covers can be rubbed to create patterned papers for use in bookmaking.

BASIC TECHNIQUE

Begin rubbing by holding or taping your paper securely in place over a textured surface, like a metal screen or plastic mat. Hold your crayon on its side so its whole length contacts the paper, and stroke the crayon or wax block over the paper, bearing down slightly to bring up the image. Vary the amount of pressure you use to create lighter or darker areas.

To produce multicolored designs, use a multicolored wax block or create a rubbing in one color and then move the paper slightly to deliberately reposition it on the rubbing surface before rubbing again with another color. Techniques and working methods will evolve as you rub over different types of surfaces. For example, I find it easier to produce an image of the horizontal lines on a rubber doormat by rubbing diagonally rather than horizontally over the piece, which seems to create too much drag on the crayon. Rubbing in any direction seems to work fine, however, on the raised bumpy pattern of a paint tray.

WHAT YOU'LL NEED

- *Paper.* Thin, hard, smooth paper and softer printmaking paper both work, although they will yield different kinds of images.

- *Rubbing wax and crayons.* Because it's very hard, rubbing wax gives a good, even distribution of color and can reproduce fine details. Even pieces of cut or folded paper can be faithfully reproduced by rubbing over them. Oldstone Rubbing Wax is available through the Daniel Smith art catalog, but only comes in black, brown, red and gold. Ordinary wax crayons, on the other hand, come in a huge range of colors and are available everywhere. Be sure to buy good quality, large, hard crayons as they are easiest to handle and most resistant to breakage. Softer crayons tend to deposit wax in clumps on some areas of the paper and skip over details in others, and some even begin to melt if they are rubbed over a surface too quickly.

  Peggy Skycraft, whose beautiful work is shown opposite, recommends using Cray-Pas or oil pastels for rubbing. She also markets her own wax pastels and multicolor wax blocks through Fascinating Folds, listed in the source directory on page 143.

- *Rubbing surfaces.* Flat surfaces with relief patterns and textures are everywhere around you. Found materials used for embossing, stenciling, and other forms of paper decorating can also be used.

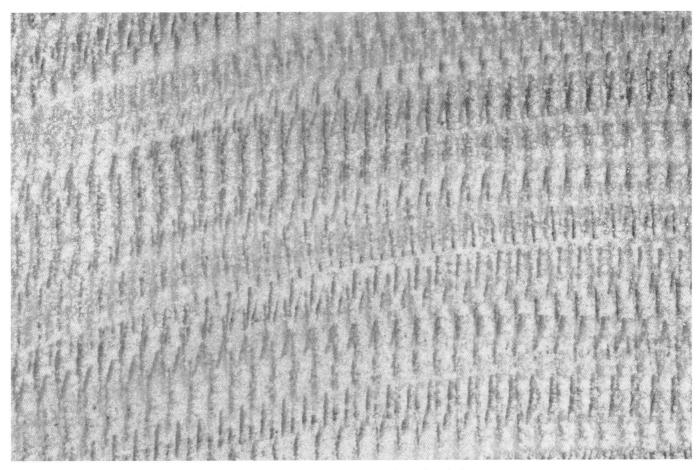

A crayon rubbing by Peggy Skycraft, created by using a multicolored wax block to rub a vinyl mat.

GOING FURTHER

This chapter cannot even begin to cover all the paper decorating techniques that can be used to create great papers for your scrapbooks and albums. You might, for example, try recycling old printed papers, such as maps, sheet music, or love letters. Enlarge or reduce designs with a photocopier and then use them to wrap hard covers or serve as background papers for photos and memorabilia. Blueprints found in the attic of an old house being renovated can become the charming cover of a scrapbook showing before and after shots of the restoration. Pages of the scrapbook could be enhanced with wallpaper swatches and copies of old newspapers found during the work. Many photocopy shops will enlarge material to poster size and, while papers that are greatly enlarged usually cease to be legible, the resulting patterns can be used to form interesting designs.

Other possible techniques incluce printmaking, paper piercing, silk-screening, watercolor and oil color marbling, Polaroid transfer techniques, and on and on. If you've tried one of the techniques mentioned in this chapter and want to pursue it further, look for books listed on page 142 that focus more specifically on that subject. Remember to experiment, too. Combining two or more paper decorating techniques on the same paper can yield some really unique designs.

CHAPTER 6

MAKING YOUR OWN PAPER

Although domestic and imported handmade papers are readily available in every imaginable color and texture, it's also fun to make your own paper for the covers and interior pages of your scrapbooks and albums. In part because materials and equipment are inexpensive and easy to purchase through papermaking supply houses and art supply stores, lots of book artists are taking time off from binding to apply their skills to papermaking. Claudia Lee, whose work is shown on page 107, has taken the opposite course: After many years of teaching papermaking and making gorgeous handmade papers for others to use, she recently began making her own albums.

Handmade papers have natural deckle edges, as shown in these papers by Jeanne Petrosky.

To begin making your own paper, you can purchase the following equipment and materials from a papermaking supplier, or improvise by using common household items.

EQUIPMENT

- *Kitchen blender.* You'll need a basic blender for macerating fiber to make the paper pulp. Purchase one to reserve for papermaking only.
- *Large dishpan or plastic storage container.* Either of these can serve as a papermaking vat. It should be about 8 inches (20 cm) deep and large enough to accommodate the mold and deckle with room to spare.
- *Mold and deckle.* The mold and matching deckle determine the size and shape of the sheet of paper made. The *mold* is the screened frame that the newly formed sheet of paper rests on, and the *deckle* rests on top of the mold to keep the pulp in place. Purchase a mold and deckle through one of the papermaking houses listed on page 143 or construct one using the diagram below.
- *Sponges.* Sponges will be used for cleanup and to help release ornery sheets from the mold.
- *Couching cloths.* Nonadhesive dressmaker's sew-in interfacing from a fabric store or old cotton sheets can be used to support newly formed sheets of paper. Cloths should be about 2 inches (5 cm) larger all around than the

paper you intend to make. Handiwipes can also be used if you don't mind the slight pattern they impart to the papers.
- *Couching felts.* Old army blankets or purchased felts will support and help draw water from the wet stack of papers. Like the couching cloths, these should be about 2 inches (5 cm) larger all around than the papers you make.
- *Press boards.* You'll need two of these, which should be made from Formica or urethaned wood, and should be slightly larger than your mold. The press boards will sandwich your *post* (a stack of couched sheets) and, with the help of some weight placed on top of them, remove most of the water from your newly formed sheets of paper. A simple paper press, made from bolts and wood (see diagram below), is the most efficient way to press a stack of wet paper.
- *Strainer and mesh curtain material.* You can use these to strain out the extra pulp at the end of your papermaking session and store it for later use.

MATERIALS

The *furnish*, or raw material from which the paper is made, can come from several sources:
- *Sheets of pulp.* Abaca (from banana leaf fibers) or cotton linters (pulp in sheet form) can be ordered from papermaking supply houses. These are easy to use and produce fine papers.

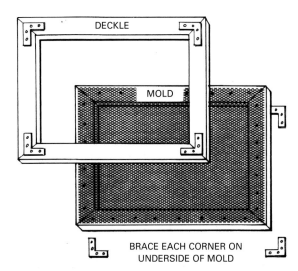

Plans for constructing a sturdy mold and deckle.

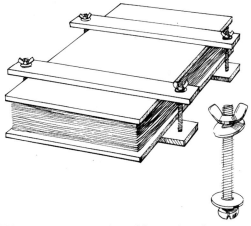

This paper press consists of four strips of waterproofed wood and bolts with wing nuts used to apply pressure to the post of papers.

BASIC TECHNIQUES

- *Recycled paper.* Computer paper, photocopy paper, old blotters, drawing paper, and mount-board can all be used to make handmade paper. Newspapers and magazines should be avoided as they are highly acidic. If you are concerned with producing papers that are archival, be especially diligent about what you use.
- *Water.* Sometimes mineral or organic compounds in water will cause brown stains to appear in a dried sheet. Use purified or distilled water for papermaking if you have high levels of minerals like iron, copper, or manganese in your tap water.
- *Inclusions.* Decorative additions like dried flowers, bits of ribbon, confetti, or threads can be added to the vat and stirred so they are floating randomly when you make a sheet of paper. They can also be added while pulping, although the flowers will no longer be whole.
- *Sizing.* Liquid sizing (available from papermaking suppliers) can be added to the pulp to make your sheets of paper less absorbent. This will be important if you want to use your hand-made papers for journals and intend to use calligraphy inks on them. An alternative is to dissolve 1 teaspoon (5 ml) gelatin in 1 cup (240 ml) boiling water and paint the mixture onto your dried sheets with a soft, wide brush.
- *Pigments and retention aid.* For vibrant, permanently colored papers, order pigments and a retention aid (to help the pigments bond to the paper fibers) from a papermaking supplier and then follow the supplier's instructions for use. You can also color your pulp by adding colored papers or fabric dyes to it.

BASIC TECHNIQUES

Although it seems miraculous, the transformation of a wet handful of pulp to a beautiful sheet of paper is quite easy. You'll first beat the *furnish*, or raw material, to a pulp and then mix the pulp with water in a vat to form a *slurry*. Next you'll dip your mold and attached deckle into the vat and lift it out, capturing some of the floating pulp. A quick shake will help form the settling fibers into a mat. After the water has drained through

the mold screen, you'll remove the deckle and transfer, or *couch*, the matted fibers onto a damp cloth. When the fibers are pressed and dried the metamorphosis will be complete and you will be rewarded with a sheet of handmade paper.

PREPARING THE PULP

Wet several linters and tear them into 1-inch (2.5-cm) pieces. Add a small handful of torn linters to a blender two-thirds full of warm water. (As a general rule of thumb, use about 1 part linters to 2 parts warm water.) Beat for 1 minute, using short bursts of speed to avoid straining the blender motor. The pulp is the proper consistency when it contains no lumps and individual fibers are suspended, cloudlike, in the water.

Empty the blended pulp into your papermaking vat and add about two more blendersful of water. Continue beating and pouring into your vat, adding more water each time, until you have about 1 pint (470 ml) of concentrated pulp mixed with 4 gallons (15 l) of water. You needn't be too concerned with exact proportions. The ratio of pulp to water can be adjusted to create thinner or thicker sheets of paper by adding more water or concentrated pulp to your vat.

If you're using recycled papers, tear light- to medium-weight papers into 1-inch (2.5-cm) pieces and soak them overnight in water. Heavy watercolor paper needs to be torn into smaller pieces and soaked for several days. For very heavy

Buckets of vividly colored pulp are constant fixtures in Claudia Lee's studio.

Adding wet, torn linters to the blender for pulping. Colored paper, dyes, or pigments can also be added to produce colored sheets.

Lowering the mold and deckle into a vat to make a sheet of paper.

Standing the mold upright at the end of the couching cloth and rolling it firmly down to release the handmade sheet.

Peeling the couching cloth off a newly formed sheet of handmade paper. The sheet will be left to dry on the Plexiglas.

paper or mountboard, an even longer soaking time or boiling may be necessary. Lightweight papers will probably only need to be beaten for about fifteen seconds, while heavier materials should be macerated longer to adequately separate the fibers.

FORMING A SHEET

Use your hand to stir and distribute the pulp throughout the water in your vat. Place the edge of your deckle on top of the screened side of your mold so that the flat edges are together. Hold the deckle in place with your thumbs and grasp the bottom of the mold with your fingers. If your mold is rectangular, place your hands on the short sides.

Hold the mold and deckle at a slight angle and lower them into the vat at its far edge, as shown at left. Then bring the mold and deckle toward you, shifting them to a horizontal position and holding them level for a moment just below the water's surface before lifting them swiftly up and out of the vat.

As the water drains through the screen, gently shake the mold and deckle from side to side and from front to back to disperse and mesh the pulp fibers you've scooped up. When most of the water has drained back into the vat, tilt the mold and deckle slightly to let additional excess water drain off. Rest your mold and deckle on the edge of the vat and carefully remove the deckle, making sure you don't drip water on your newly formed sheet of paper. If you do drip water on the sheet, which may cause a thin spot or hole, or if your first sheet appears too thick or thin in one area, place the mold pulp-side down on the surface of the pulp-and-water mixture to "kiss off" the sheet back into the vat.

The smooth, continuous motion that produces a uniform sheet of paper will come with a little practice. Judging how much pulp to add to the water in your vat will also come with experience. In general, if your paper seems too thick, add more water to the vat. If it's too thin (as it will be after you've made several sheets), add more beaten pulp.

COUCHING

After you've removed the deckle from the mold, it's time to *couch* (rhymes with "pooch") the sheet. Couching (from the French term *coucher*, which means "to lay down") refers to the act of transferring the newly formed sheet of paper from the mold to the dampened couching cloth or felt.

To prepare a couching pad, place a dampened felt on your urethaned press board and a dampened piece of couching cloth on top of the felt, smoothing out any wrinkles in the cloth. Stand your mold upright at the cloth's edge and roll the mold firmly down onto it, as shown opposite. When the opposite edge of the mold contacts the cloth, lift the first edge up. Usually this slight rocking motion releases the sheet of paper. If you have difficulty getting the paper to release at first, place the mold face down on the couching cloth and use a wet sponge to press and release the back of the sheet through the mold screen.

When the sheet is successfully couched, dampen another couching cloth and place it on top of the wet sheet of paper. Your next piece of handmade paper will be couched on top of this cloth. To build up a stack, or post, of papers, continue couching and adding dampened cloths until you've created a stack of about ten sheets. Then add another thick felt to the top of the stack and cover it with the other press board.

PRESSING AND DRYING

The simplest way to press the water from your post is to stand on the top press board for about ten minutes and then lay a couple of bricks on the board to finish the job. If you'd rather not be caught standing around when there are scrapbooks to be made, you can make a simple paper press like the one shown on page 104 (which can be used to press books as well). C-clamps can also be placed on the stack and tightened to press out moisture. Regardless of which method you choose, be sure to elevate the post of papers in a larger tub or kitty litter pan (if you're not outside or near a floor drain) to allow the water to drain away.

When most of the moisture has been pressed out of your handmade papers, transfer them to a flat drying surface such as glass, Plexiglas, or Formica. Transport each sheet on its couching cloth and use a wide, flat brush to gently brush the back of the cloth to coax the sheet onto the drying surface. Then peel off the couching cloth, as shown opposite (bottom). Allow the sheet to remain in position until it is completely dry. You can also pin each couching cloth, with a damp handmade sheet still attached, to Styrofoam or urethaned wood (to minimize shrinkage) and let the sheets air-dry. A third alternative, if you just can't wait, is to place each pressed sheet between blotters and iron it dry.

Once the sheets of handmade paper are dry, they can be stacked and put under some books or boards for several days to flatten them. The sheets will then be ready for use in bookmaking.

Claudia Lee created the cover of this art album with her handmade papers. The interior consists of large envelopes designed to hold an assortment of her handmade sheets.

Learning to make a sheet of paper is only one aspect of the papermaking adventures you can enjoy. When you've made your fill of colorful, thick, substantial sheets for soft book covers and crisp, thin sheets for journal pages, it is time to experiment with other papermaking techniques.

An accordion-fold book by Jeanne Petrosky. Jeanne couched the pages directly on top of one another, letting the spines and fore edges of alternating pages bond together.

MAKING BOOKS DIRECTLY FROM THE VAT

Although an accordion-fold book can be made by gluing the edges of handmade papers together, books like the one shown at left (made by Jeanne Petrosky) can also be made right from the vat, by couching directly on top of the previously-made sheet of paper. Because wet sheets of handmade paper will bond to each other, Jeanne slips a couching cloth between the sheets wherever she doesn't want the papers to adhere.

WET EMBOSSING

If you press some of the water out of newly made papers, place them on top of a textured surface, cover them with a couching cloth, and roll over them with a rolling pin, you can "wet emboss" them with raised decorative patterns that are perfect for use on book covers and pages. Unmounted rubber stamps, sheets of textured flooring, and decorative tiles can all be used this way to impart texture to handmade sheets.

If you want to emboss scattered materials that would be disturbed if you rolled over them, place materials like lace, string, and beans onto a waterproofed press board, lay your pressed handmade

This wet-embossed handmade paper, which was made by pressing a newly formed sheet of paper onto a wooden batik stamp, makes the perfect frame for pressed flowers.

TECHNIQUES

paper on top of the materials, and cover the paper with a dampened couching felt. Top the stack with another press board and apply pressure. Objects with low relief, like keys or a small pair of scissors, can also be embossed in this way. Leave the materials in place until the sheet dries to impart their texture and patterns to the paper.

PAPER CASTING

Paper casting is a great way to create lightweight yet very dramatic relief sculptures for book covers or pages. By casting pulp into a mold or over an armature, such as cookie molds or paper casting molds (available from papermaking and art supply stores), you can create paper with a specific shape and depth. (To explore making plasticine or plaster paper casting molds based on your own designs, consult one of the books devoted solely to papermaking, listed on page 142.)

Additives like methyl cellulose and wallpaper paste can be mixed with your pulp (1 teaspoon [5 ml] per blenderful of pulp) to create stronger paper castings, but may also make it more difficult to release the dried pulp from molds made of anything other than plastic. If you use an additive (and are not casting in a plastic mold), spray your mold with a commercial release agent or nonstick cooking spray, or rub it with a small amount of Vaseline, before filling it with pulp.

To begin casting, mix some pulp in your blender or lift pulp from your vat and place it in a strainer to remove some of the water. Use your hands to press the pulp evenly into a mold, letting some of it extend over the edges to create a deckle that will help the casting integrate with other papers on your book cover. Apply pressure with a damp sponge, as shown above right, to wick out some of the moisture. Wring the sponge out as you work to remove as much moisture as possible.

When the casting is dry, peel it from the mold. If necessary, use a dull knife to help it release. You can then glue it onto a supportive paper or another paper to form an ornament for an album cover. Castings can be made in their natural color or with different colored pulps to create a variegated piece.

Making a cast-paper dinosaur in a purchased cookie mold.

A cast-paper design by Christopher Miller forms the perfect decoration for the cover of a garden journal.

CHAPTER 7

WORKING WITH PHOTOS

Photographs add immeasurably to scrapbook and album pages. They can jog your memory in later years and give future generations a glimpse of their relatives and the worlds in which they lived. They can also communicate much about the personality of the person who took the photos and made the album, depending upon how casual or formal the photos are.

While it is, of course, important to take your photographs with a quality camera and to know something about composition, it's also important to know how to present and mount your photos on the page. The techniques that follow will show you how to isolate important parts of a shot by cropping, how to color your photos so as to maintain the romantic mood or historic theme of a scrapbook, and how to mount them in keeping with the casual or formal flavor of your book. You'll also learn how to make decorative accents like stamped, calligraphic, and layered paper borders to unify photographs on a page and show off individual shots to their advantage.

Detail of a scrapbook page by Janet Hofacker. (Full image shown on page 118.)

DESIGNING THE PAGE

If you're working with only a few photos per page, it's usually fairly easy to create a well-balanced page layout. But if you're working on a larger scale, with many photos on each page, and you don't have a graphic design background, chances are you may feel a bit intimidated by the task ahead. It may help to look through upscale magazines to see how professional designers lay out photo spreads, and to check out some books on graphic design. The general suggestions provided in the "Working with Color" and "Collage" sections (pages 56 and 58, respectively) will also help you create a unified work.

CROPPING

The best place to begin cropping new photographs is in the viewfinder of your camera, before you actually take the picture. Take a moment to really consider what you want the focus of your photograph to be. One photographer friend notes that many people take pictures of family as though they were shooting pictures of a snake: from as far away as possible. Sure, you can have the photo enlarged, but definition and clarity will suffer. If your photography skills are less than good, it pays to borrow a book on portrait, action, or nature photography, or to take a course at a local college or art center. Your local photography shop can also be a valuable resource. In addition to helping you find the proper camera to suit your needs and level of expertise, they usually have staff who will look at your shots and offer constructive suggestions.

Extreme cropping works well to isolate an image on the cover of this scrapbook, designed by Roberta Altshuler.

If you're working with existing photos, or copies of photos, the decision of how and where to crop will depend on your personal whims and the compostion of the entire page. Some people like to crop shots and overlap them to form a photomontage. You can even purchase grids at photography and crafts supply shops that will show you how to crop groups of photos so that they fit together like a puzzle. Other folks like to silhouette-cut their photos so that no background remains, as on the cover shown opposite. This technique can be effective when used judiciously.

Be aware, however, that what seems like extraneous background detail can sometimes be interesting to future generations viewing the album. The image of my 1966 Volkswagen Beetle, captured in the background of one shot, has become more important to me than the family gathering the photo was meant to document. Likewise, a photo of my mother holding a large monkey at Monkey Jungle in Florida wouldn't be half as much fun if someone had cropped out the sign in the background (noticed after the photo was taken) that reads: "Caution! Do not handle monkeys—all monkeys bite."

TINTING BLACK-AND-WHITE PHOTOS

An easy way to add color to black-and-white photos is by hand-coloring them with dye-filled pens, like Spot Pens. These pens come in large and small starter sets that include colored pens, a premoistening solution to help photos absorb the dyes, a dye remover pad (for mistakes), and a sponge to apply the solution. The technique is really quite simple and effective for accenting small areas of a photo. Just apply the moistening solution over a small area until your print is tacky, then use the pen to apply color in a light, circular motion.

Some artists, like Sarah Wagner Ranes, whose precise, allover coloring of a black-and-white photo is pictured above right, prefer to work with Marshall Photo Oils and colored pencils to achieve a more painterly quality. Because the oils

can be mixed to create different shades and nuances of color, they allow for more versatility. Working on a matte-surface paper (because the oil color needs a "tooth" to adhere to), Sarah first uses colored pencils and then layers over them with a delicate palette of Marshall oils, using cotton swabs to apply the oils and cotton balls to blend them. She also uses a vinyl eraser to remove color from specific areas. After the oils have dried, which can take several days, Sarah goes back in with colored pencils to add detail and highlight or soften areas of the photo.

Sarah Wagner Ranes used photo oils and colored pencils to color this black-and-white photograph.

Sarah also sometimes alters her photos by sepia-toning them, as shown in the images below (left). The brownish cast of the finished prints makes them look like antique photos. She begins by taking her photos on infrared film and printing them on Agfa Portriga paper. She then treats them to a Kodak Sepia Toner two-part bath: Part one bleaches the photos, and part two develops the brown tones. Many photo shops can similarly alter your black-and-white shots to "age" them.

MOUNTING

To mount your photographs, use decorative paper mats as previously mentioned (see page 64) or use a reversible glue made especially for the task. Other options include using photo corners to hold photos in place, or placing them in slits cut right into the album page, as shown below (right), or in a mat to be adhered to the page.

Many types of photo corners are available, including clear, self-adhesive ones that tend to disappear from view (which is especially useful if your photo album has different colored pages). There are also the standard black, white, silver, and gold photo corners, along with colorful ones bearing tiny pictures of flowers and other motifs. Check for these in photo shops. Elegant laser-cut corners, such as those shown opposite (bottom), look especially good with antique photos and can be purchased from catalogs such as Light Impressions. If you are concerned about the life-span of your album, make sure photo corners and other materials are of archival quality.

If you want to create your own photo corners, make a pattern by clipping off a corner of an envelope, opening it and trimming it to size, and then tracing around it. You can also make a pattern by first cutting out an "L"-shaped piece of

Sepia-toning can be used to make black-and-white prints look like antique photos, as in this work by Sarah Wagner.

By cutting slits into a page or backing paper and tucking the corners of a photo into the slits, photos can be held in place and easily removed from an album.

paper (composed of three squares in an "L" shape), then folding the two outside squares back and gluing them down. Slip the finished corners over the edges of a photo and then glue them in place on your album page. More decorative corners can be made by cutting them out with edging scissors, or by punching them with tiny holes. Stamp companies also make rubber-stamp corner templates that you can use to create photo corners. Try embossing (with a heat gun or an embossing plate) and hand coloring the interiors of the stamped designs for lots of options.

Finally, Roberta Altshuler has devised a novel way to attach photos to album pages: by using eyelets (available in craft stores) to attach photos both to the page and each other. Although certainly not an archival or reversible way to mount photos, this is a fun way to create a casual album with expanding photo galleries, as shown at right.

Roberta Altshuler used eyelet attachments in this scrapbook to create a playful device that expands to reveal a set of photos.

Elegant laser-cut photo corners complement the antique look of this scrapbook page by Janet Hofacker. Pigment inks were brushed across the page to create a color wash background. (Stamp designs by Stamp Francisco.)

Although many of the paper decorating and paper art techniques previously mentioned can be used to decorate photo album pages, there are a few additional techniques that work particularly well for accenting photos, and deserve special mention here.

STAMPED BORDERS

By stamping interlocking designs onto a sheet of heavy paper and using an X-acto knife to cut out all but the stamped design, you can create a great raised frame for a photo. Roberta Altshuler, whose album page is shown below, uses this technique to accent and effectively crop her photos at the same time. There are also lots of large rubber stamps made especially for framing photos. And roller stamps, which produce a continuous design, can be used to create borders as well.

LAYERED PAPER BORDERS

A different type of border can be made by first using edging scissors or the Art Deckle (see opposite) to alter the edges of purchased or handmade papers, then layering the paper and placing the photo on top. You may want to use a decorative corner punch on the edges of the photo (or on a copy of the photo) as well, to continue the design.

TIP

Many people find it difficult to work with the short blades found on edging scissors. It's easier to cut a continuous design if you don't use the entire length of the scissor blade. Cut only part of the way, then move the paper you're cutting so that the pattern on the paper matches the tooth pattern on the scissor blade.

Roberta Altshuler cut out stamped designs to create this frame, which both accents and crops her photo.

DECKLE-EDGE MATS

Although you can create deckle edges as described in earlier chapters—by wetting and tearing paper against the edge of a conventional metal ruler, or by tearing it away from itself—the results can be spotty, especially when creating inner openings in paper mats. Instead, try Design A Card's Art Deckle (available in art supply stores), which will reliably create photo mats with softly frayed edges that resemble those on handmade paper. To deckle the outside of a paper mat, simply lay your paper face down and, using an upward motion, remove a 1/2-inch (1.3-cm) strip from the edge of the paper by pulling it over the teeth of the Art Deckle. Continue to deckle all four edges of your paper.

To create a deckled inner opening for your mat, trace or measure and draw a square or rectangle on the back of your paper. (An added bonus of the Art Deckle is the zero at the center of its ruled markings, which makes centering easy.) Using an X-acto knife, cut x-shaped slits to create paper flaps, as explained on page 63. Hold your Art Deckle on the lines that mark the edges of the opening and pull each paper flap over its teeth, as shown at right. Even circular and oval mats can be created

if you trace the size opening you want and tear the paper in small sections over the teeth of the tool.

If you want to create deckle edges on a mat made from heavier paper, use a brush to lay a line of water along the edges of the paper, wait a minute or so, then proceed to pull the paper over the teeth of the Art Deckle.

DIE-CUT PAPERS

If you have access to a die-cutting tool or can visit a local frame shop, you can have your pages die cut. Shereen La Plantz created the delightful

Pulling paper over the teeth of the Art Deckle to create a photo mat with softly frayed edges that resemble the deckle edges on handmade paper.

I couldn't wait to begin filling this photo album, created by Shereen La Plantz. Her die-cut pages fold up from the bottom and are glued together along the left side to securely hold pictures—a page design that can be adapted to many album styles.

photo album pictured on page 117 by die cutting pages before folding them into position (the fold is at the bottom of the page) and then stitching the pages together to form a book. A handheld circular cutting tool can also be used to create pages with shaped openings for photos.

CREATIVE FRAMING

There are many ways you can frame photos to present them in a formal or more casual style. Try cutting strips of decorative paper and arranging them to form a frame. You can also adhere horizontal strips of paper to adhesive film and then cut the paper vertically to produce thin multicolored strips that can be placed around a photo. Edges can be overlapped or mitered if you wish to create a closed rectangle. Janet Hofacker, whose work is shown below, applied dimensional paint around the edges of her photo to accent and crop it; metallic foil can be similarly used to create a decorative frame (see cover by Susan Pickering Rothamel, shown on page 59).

Janet Hofacker used dimensional fabric paint to accent and crop the photo shown. (Victorian stamp by Stampington & Company.)

CALLIGRAPHIC DESIGNS

Repetitive calligraphic designs, like the ones shown below by Jean Marie Seaton, make striking borders for photos. Although Jean Marie's calligraphic expertise (the result of years of training) would be hard to match, you'd be surprised at how easy it is to create pleasing photo borders using a chisel-edged pen.

Begin by holding the pen at a 45-degree angle to your paper. With your wrist locked, pull the pen toward you to make a series of strokes, each the same height and distance apart. Be as consistent as possible as you repeat each mark. Play with the pen, trying to duplicate some of Jean Marie's curves and zigzags to see how changing the angle of the pen affects the mark. In time you will be able to transfer your designs to album pages to create beautiful borders for your photographs. In addition, the exercise of repeating strokes will help you slow down and fine-tune your writing, which will help when making journal, scrapbook, or album entries. (See also Chapter 8, "Creative Lettering.")

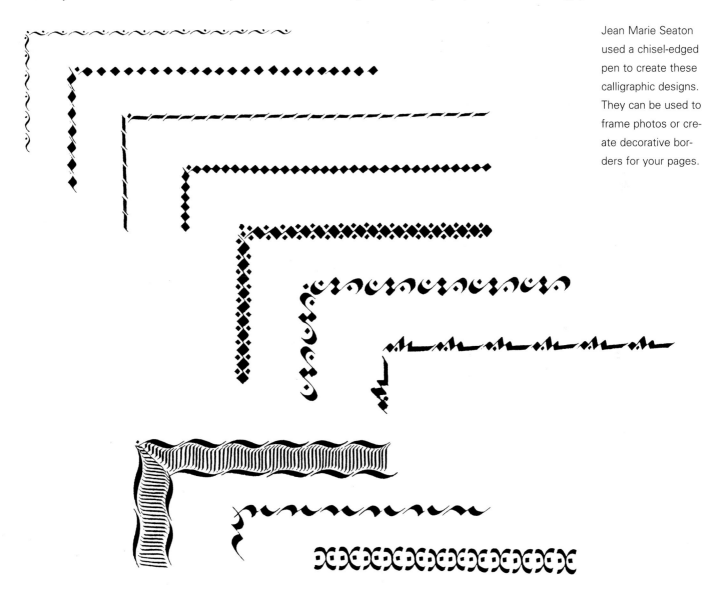

Jean Marie Seaton used a chisel-edged pen to create these calligraphic designs. They can be used to frame photos or create decorative borders for your pages.

CREATIVE LETTERING

Although many book artists prefer to let the artwork on their books' covers suggest what the books are about, others like to clearly state what's inside. If you are not a calligrapher, or are among the many afflicted with poor handwriting, the prospect of even adding a title to your journal or album can seem daunting. (If you are an accomplished calligrapher, you don't need to read this section; you already possess what most of us envy: beautiful handwriting.)

The suggestions that follow include ways to improve your handwriting, guidelines from professional calligraphers on how to do creative lettering for book titles and pages, and finally, if you're a "lost lefty" like me, ways to cheat by using stamps, stencils, tracing techniques, and computer lettering.

Formal calligraphy and watercolors grace the pages of Pam McKee's art journal. This page contains ideas for planting ivy and creating a shadow box of wedding mementos.

IMPROVING YOUR HANDWRITING

Art journals often use just pictures to tell a story. But if you want to use a journal in a more conventional sense—to recount your dreams, travels, and observations on the world—or simply to add the necessary who, what, where, and when to your scrapbook pages, you'll want to make sure that your handwriting is legible.

The first suggestion for improving your handwriting is to *slow down*. Our fast-paced lives have made most of us speed-writers, and the increased speed often results in letters that collapse into each other. If you have access to a personal letter or journal you wrote ten or so years ago you may be amazed, as I was, to see how your handwriting has changed—for the worse. In my own case, I've adopted the nasty habit of making some letters — R, for instance—three different ways, depending on which letter they are attached to and how quickly I can make the attachment. When I look back over my earlier handwriting, when I printed

letters without such elaborate attachments (which was more like drawing them), I find that my writing was much more legible. Yes it took longer, but it looked better and didn't produce the writer's cramp my speed-writing does.

LETTERING TOOLS

I notice that my writing changes according to the type of writing implement I use. For some reason, pencil always looks good, while fine-tipped pens look sloppy. I do my best lettering with a wide-nibbed fountain pen. It's a good idea to play with several kinds of pens to find the one that feels most comfortable. Another trick is to write on a padded surface, which will help the pen glide more smoothly than it would on a hard desktop, which may have any number of imperfections.

The following basic materials are recommended for lettering in your scrapbooks, albums, and journals:

Peggy Johnston's personal, yet very legible, handwriting makes it easy to read her travel journal.

- *Pens.* The ZIG "Memory System," widely available in photography and crafts supply stores, is a group of archival-quality pens filled with pigment ink that is acid-free, lightfast, waterproof, fade-proof, and nonbleeding—perfect for scrapbooking and journaling. The ZIG Writer, which has a bullet tip at one end and a fine tip at the other, is a favorite for all lettering styles. The ZIG Opaque Writer is perfect for writing on and decorating dark or bright papers; it comes in many colors, including white, silver, and gold. The system also includes ZIG Emboss Pens, which are fun to use when you want embossed or raised letters, as well as dual-tip calligraphy pens, scroll pens (which have a split tip for making double lines), and brush pens.
- *Colored pencils.* Memory Pencils, distributed by EK Success, are ideal for shading and shadowing and come in a wide variety of colors, including primary, earth, and pastel colors.
- *Ruler.* The C-Thru Ruler Company makes a ruler that has a grid imprinted on the front, which makes drawing lines so much easier. It is also wonderful for making evenly spaced slanted lines across your page. Get the 18-inch (46-cm) rather than the 12-inch (30-cm) style.
- *Pencil.* A good mechanical pencil, ideally with a no. 2 lead, will give you a nice crisp line and will not dull as easily as a regular pencil.
- *Eraser.* A kneaded or oblong white eraser should be used; they erase cleaner and with less smudging than other erasers.
- *Compass.* A compass is used in various lettering techniques for drawing curves and circles.

- *Tracing paper.* You'll need tracing paper for tracing letters from source material and in various creative lettering techniques.
- *Transfer paper.* When placed under tracing paper, transfer paper will allow you to use a pencil to transfer creative lettering to your page.

THE ITALIC HAND

Although the best way to learn calligraphy is to sign up for a course and be prepared to practice diligently, the following section offers a few tips and techniques that can help you design titles and page headings without sacrificing the personality of your own handwriting. Carole Maurer, a nationally known calligrapher (no relation to me), teaches a course in which she offers a number of suggestions to help noncalligraphers. She suggests that people who need to transform illegible handwriting should learn a simple italic hand. The advice and lettering examples that follow were provided by Carole. As she explains:

> *The italic hand is much easier to learn than the rigid, mechanical "ball and stick" method of printing most of us were taught in grade school. Also, with this system there is no need for the difficult transition from manuscript [printing] to "real" writing [cursive]. Instead, the italic [lower case] forms are simply joined together via entries and exits to form a cursive hand. The capitals, too, are much simpler than the ones with curves and loops taught today.*

As Carole explains, one benefit of the italic hand is that ascender and descender letters are drawn without loops, which can cause illegibility. Letters are based on an ellipse, not a circle, and should be

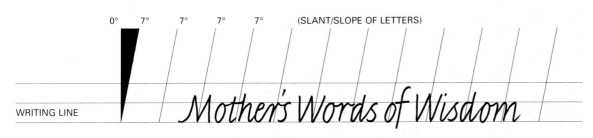

An example of the italic hand. Notice how italic letters are based on an ellipse, not a circle.

consistently sloped (slanted)—about 5 to 10 degrees from the vertical. Because italic letters can be unjoined, joined, or freely written, they still allow your own personality, style, and flair to come through in your writing.

Natural breathing places (pen lifts) appear in words after certain letters, but because italic letters are different shapes, the spaces between them cannot be measured exactly. Instead, you have to adjust the amount of white space between letters so they *appear* the same. Generally speaking, any two straight letters should be the farthest apart, a straight letter and a curved letter should be closer together, and two adjacent curved letters should be the closest of all. A certain amount of visual judgment is required to space your letters correctly. It may be helpful to look at your lettering upside down or from a distance for a fresh perspective. If a "hole" appears within a word, it means that the letters are too far apart; a dark area means that the letters are too close together. With practice, you will be able to judge the right spacing by eye.

The italic hand is easy to learn and less likely than other lettering styles to break down when you write rapidly. Once mastered, it will restore your ability to write gracefully and legibly. For

> **TIP**
>
> It is important to establish a rhythm in your writing. Try practicing to music with a heavy beat, which will not only be enjoyable but will help your writing acquire a rhythm.

more information on the italic hand, refer to one of the many books on the market that focus specifically on handwriting, some of which are listed on page 142.

Modern italic can be written with a variety of instruments, but looks particularly nice when written with a cartridge ink pen or fountain pen with a broad edge. Broad pen italic calligraphy, which is written with a square-edged nib, fountain pen, or marker, uses the same letterforms as the skeletal version described above—the trick is in the pen angle. The thick and thin strokes of the letters so characteristic of italic calligraphy depend on the angle at which the nib meets the paper in relation to the writing line (usually 45 degrees for italic). With a few exceptions, the nib should be held at a constant angle, as illustrated opposite (bottom).

Unjoined letters written at a 7-degree slope. "X-height" refers to the body height of each letter. Notice the consistency of the letters' size and slope.

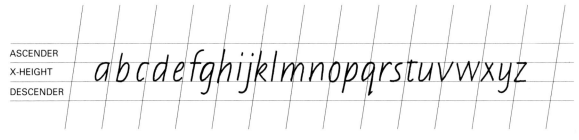

ASCENDER
X-HEIGHT
DESCENDER

abcdefghijklmnopqrstuvwxyz

Joined letters written at a 7-degree slope. There are no loops in ascender and descender letters (as in cursive) that tend to cause illegibility.

ASCENDER
X-HEIGHT
DESCENDER

abcdefghijklmnopqrstuvwxyz

ASCENDER
X-HEIGHT
DESCENDER

Favorite Ethnic Restaurants

Joined letters, again written at a 7-degree slope. Notice how natural breathing places (pen lifts) appear in the words after certain letters.

ASCENDER
X-HEIGHT
DESCENDER

a d g q · n h m u y · o c e · b p

Unjoined letters, written at a 7-degree slope. Many italic letters have the same shape—more than in most lettering styles—which makes the alphabet easier to learn.

ASCENDER
X-HEIGHT
DESCENDER

Art Journal   Art Journal   Art Journal

The italic hand allows your own personality, style, and flair to come through, as shown here in the different styles of unjoined *(left)*, joined *(center)*, and freely written *(right)* words.

45°

WRITING LINE

7°   7°   7°   7°   (SLANT/SLOPE OF LETTERS)

in io   nine

Photos

When lettering with a square-edged nib, the pen should be held at a constant angle to form the thick and thin strokes of italic calligraphy.

LETTERING STYLES

The following creative lettering styles were suggested by Carole for use on book covers and pages. Most are easy to master and can readily disguise a less-than-perfect lettering ability. Be sure to practice any new style on scrap paper before trying it on your bound book pages. Or, to be safest, transfer your letters using the tracing methods described on page 131.

ABCDEFGHIJKLMNOPQRSTUVWXYZ

ABCDEFGHIJKLMNOPQRSTUVWXYZ

BIRD WATCHING ON LONG POND

BIRD WATCHING ON LONG POND

Narrow caps.

CHRISTMAS 1999

A

CHRISTMAS 1999

B

CHRISTMAS 1999

C

CHRISTMAS 1999

D

Outlined letters.

NARROW CAPS

Lightly draw pencil guidelines to keep the tops and bottoms of the letters flush, as shown at left. You may also need to draw a few vertical lines to keep your letters straight. Try to keep all letters about the same width, with the exception of *I* and *J*, which will be narrower, and *M* and *W*, which will be a little wider. (The curved parts of letters will also extend slightly outside the guidelines.) Try using different marker weights and rendering more casual (but not sloppy!) letters, as appropriate.

OUTLINES

To outline your letters, first write each letter in pencil, spacing a little more between letters than you normally would. Then ink over the pencil lines with a marker (Figure A, below left). Draw around each letter with a different color, keeping edges sharp and leaving equal amounts of white space around the letters (approximately $1/8$ inch [0.3 cm], depending on the size of your letters). Erase any pencil lines that still show (Figure B, below left).

A rounder outline can be created by following the same process as above but rounding the edges of the outlines (Figure C, below left). For "puffy" letters, leave even more white space around the letters and then use black ink to make fat, round outlines. Erase the original pencil lines and color in the letters. Space letters closer together if you want an overlapping effect, as in Figure D, below left.

DROP SHADOWS

To create drop shadows, first trace over a letter or words with a strip of tracing paper. Place a piece of transfer paper on your book page and tape the tracing paper over it, then use a hard pencil to trace your letters (Figure A-1, opposite). Move the tracing paper *slightly* so your outlines are just to the left of and below the letters (or to the right of and above or below the letters, depending on which way you want the shadows to drop). Trace over the letters again (Figure A-2, opposite). Then remove the tracing and transfer papers and fill in the shadows (Figure A-3, opposite). A darker shade can be very effective for this technique.

You can also try using a calligraphy marker to make drop shadows, as shown in Figures B, C, and D, below. For downstrokes, hold the pen at a zero-degree angle (horizontally) and pull it straight down. For cross-strokes, hold the marker at a 90-degree angle (vertically), pulling it straight across.

STAGGERED LETTERS

To form staggered letters, like those shown below (bottom), lightly draw a straight horizontal pencil line to use as a guide. Then draw letters above and below the line, turning them at different angles to achieve a playful, tumbling look.

LETTERS ON A WAVE

Use a pencil to lightly draw two parallel, gentle curves on a piece of card-weight paper, as shown on page 128. Then cut along the curves with scissors or an X-acto knife. (Be sure to mark the piece's top and bottom so you don't accidentally reverse the curves.) With repositionable tape, attach the piece to the paper you want to write on. Draw a light pencil line, following the curve along the bottom of the piece. Then remove the piece and place its top edge above the line you've just drawn, so it rests at the desired height of your letters. Draw another light pencil line, following the curve along the top of the piece. Flexible tubelike curves and plastic curve templates may also be helpful. (If you're not as concerned about accurate spacing, you can simply draw the original curves directly onto your "good" paper.) Now lightly pencil in slant lines so you know how much to make the letters lean

Drop shadows.

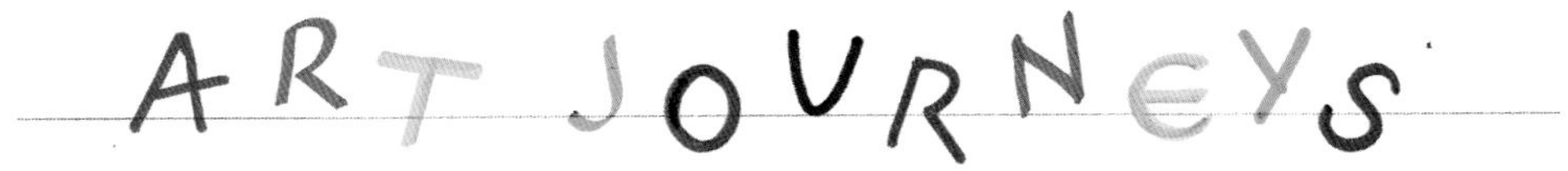

A   TRAVELS
1

TRAVELS   TRAVELS
2   3

B   TRAVELS

C   TRAVELS

D   TRAVELS

Staggered letters.

ART JOURNEYS

127

(see Figure A, below). Turn the paper as you write, letting the letters go back and forth on the curve, but always staying within the two lines (Figure B, below). You can also keep the letters straight up and down for a different effect. When you are satisfied with the letters, trace over them in ink and erase all pencil lines.

LETTERS ON A CURVE

Draw two circles with a compass, one inside the other, with the difference between the two outlines the same as the desired height of your letters. Use a ruler to draw radiating lines from the center of the circles to the outermost circumference, as shown below. Draw as many lines as you need—they will serve as guidelines for slanting your letters around the curve. Starting at any point on the circle, align your letters with the guidelines, turning the paper as you write. When you're finished, find the center of the writing by tracing it onto tracing paper and then folding the paper over so the first and last letters fall on top of one another; whichever letter falls on the fold of the paper is in the center. You can either create the letters directly on your scrapbook page and estimate which letter should fall in the center, or create them on another piece of paper and either paste them in or use tracing techniques to transfer

Letters written on
a wave.

Letters written on
a curve.

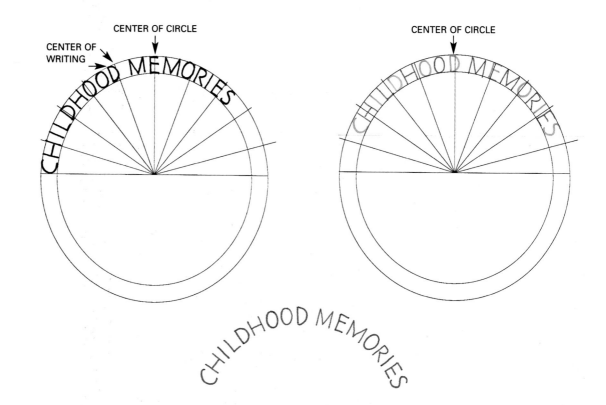

them to your page. Trace over your finished letters in ink, then erase all pencil lines.

When I asked Paul Maurer, another calligrapher (no relation to Carole), for his tips on creative lettering, he made many of the same suggestions as Carole. He also mentioned comic books as good sources for layouts and lettering styles. Try tracing letters and phrases from them as well as from calligraphy books.

Paul sent some delightful work that shows how lettering and doodles made with colored felt-tip pens can combine to create playful book cover art. The felt-tip pen designs, he added, can also help novices camouflage problems with letter spacing.

Paul Maurer, a well-known calligrapher, often departs from formal lettering to create playful cover art with colored felt-tip pens, as shown in these three covers. The lettering treatment for the cover above was based on comic book art.

If your lettering is to be used in a scrapbook, photo album, or journal that contains mostly drawings and collage, there are many options besides hand lettering or cutting words out of magazines ransom-note style. Try some of the techniques that follow, which include using rubber stamps, stencils, and computer lettering, to add creative titles and text to your books.

Rubber stamps are available in large and small alphabets and different typefaces, some made to be linked and lined up to each other to create words, others to be stamped individually. Often it's more expressive and fun to sprinkle the letters over the page in an artfully haphazard fashion. You can lightly pencil positioning marks if you feel safer doing so, or let serendipity be your guide. You can also draw wavy lines and arcs on which to stamp the letters, as shown for hand lettering on page 128. Another option is to stamp letters on heavy paper, then cut them out and arrange them across the page. This way you can move the letters around and try different ways of positioning them before permanently gluing them in place. Roberta Altshuler used this technique to advantage on her Alaskan scrapbook cover, shown on page 112. Letters that have been thermal embossed also look especially good on book covers.

Brass and plastic stencils offer a second way to letter scrapbook pages. As with all the techniques described here, you can either work directly on the page or create your letters on paper that coordinates with your album page, later transferring them to your "good" page. Stencil paints in various colors can be used, or you can use embossing pens.

Computer lettering makes it easy to create yet another type of attractive lettering for albums. Because there are so many typefaces available, it's easy to choose a lettering style that coordinates with your book subject, whether it be casual and humorous or sophisticated and formal. Photocopy shops can usually provide you with many styles of

This page from one of Janet Hofacker's art journals shows how effective stamping in a wavy pattern can be.

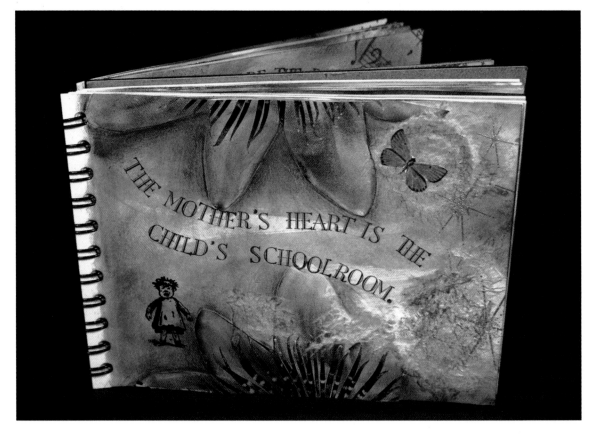

Computer lettering used by Susan Rothamel blends well with the other elements on this scrapbook page.

lettering, and feed information directly to a photocopy machine that then prints out your text on various types and weights of paper.

Carole Maurer has offered the following method for tracing, positioning, and transferring computer lettering (or lettering from other sources) onto your page:

1. On a piece of tracing paper, draw a pencil line to serve as a base for the letters you wish to copy. Place the tracing paper over the letters to be transferred and carefully trace them with a sharp pencil.

2. Turn the tracing paper over and use a soft pencil to scribble over the *back* of the traced letters. Dab up the excess pencil carbon with a tissue to prevent smearing. Turn the paper over so that the clean side is facing you.

3. Use a transparent ruler to draw a light pencil base line on your album page where you want the letters to appear. Position the tracing paper, with the clean side facing up, on the line you just drew and use removable tape to hold it in place. Using a sharp pencil, trace over the letters again. The carbon on the back of the tracing paper will transfer the letters onto your paper in light pencil marks. Remove the tracing paper and go over the letters with a marker, making adjustments to the letters as necessary.

If you practice Carole's technique on scrap paper first, you'll soon be able to use it directly on your scrapbook and album pages. But try not to overdo your reliance on tracing; once your handwriting has reached a consistently legible level (mine improved as soon as I learned to make those Rs), you should try using it in your books. One of the most interesting things about looking back over your books in years to come will be recognizing your personality not only in what you wrote, but in how you wrote it.

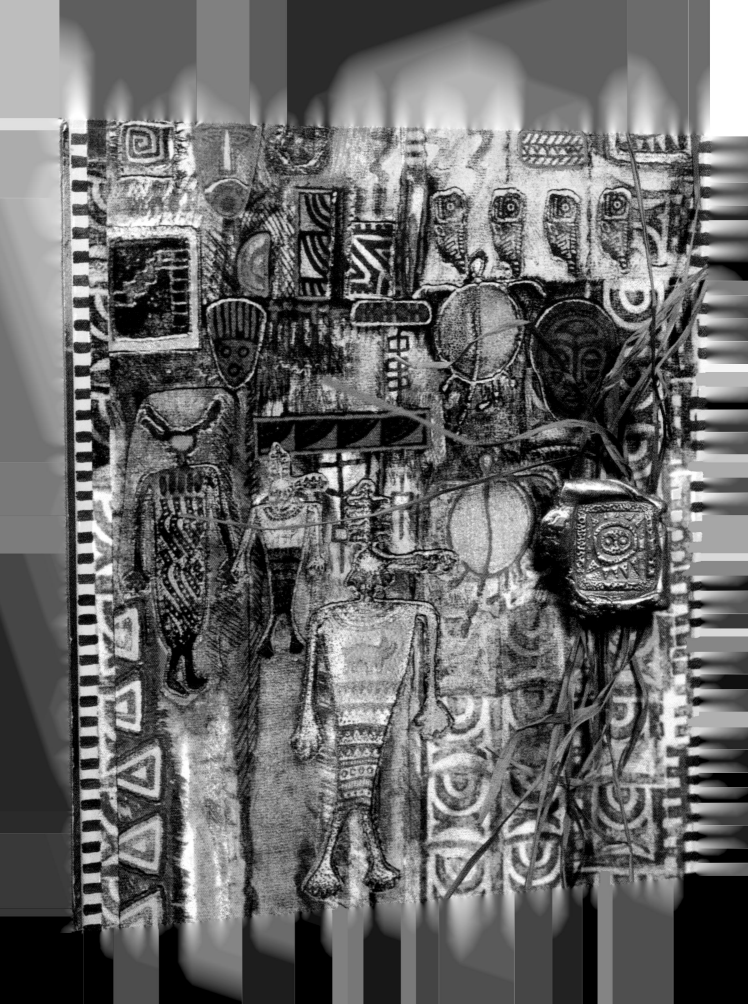

CHAPTER 9

A SCRAPBOOK GALLERY

When most people first begin bookmaking, they tend to be too concerned with technique to produce works that are really expressive. As confidence grows, however, they concentrate more on cover and page design, take more creative risks, and make more exciting works. This gallery is designed to inspire you to create your own innovative and original books.

Sherrill Kahn used scanned images of her painted fabrics to create a collage cover for this book, which is accented with Play-Doh and raffia.

Memory Book,
by Rob Bostick.
Computer circuit
board cover with
an actual piano
hinge spine.

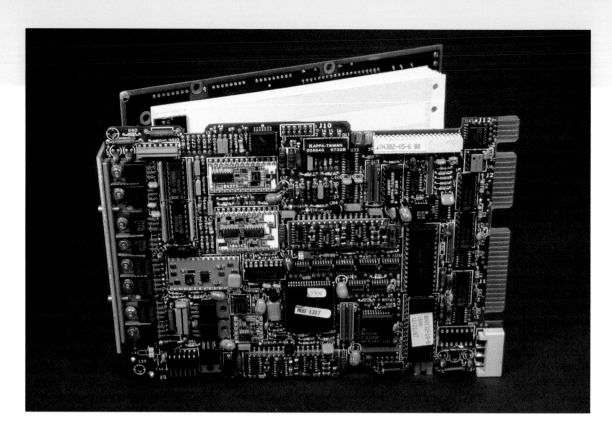

A Road Alphabet, by Nancy Leavitt. Three identical single-signature sewn accordion-fold bindings are shown: *top,* opened out completely; *bottom right,* partially open; and *bottom left,* in the closed position. Painting over offset printing.

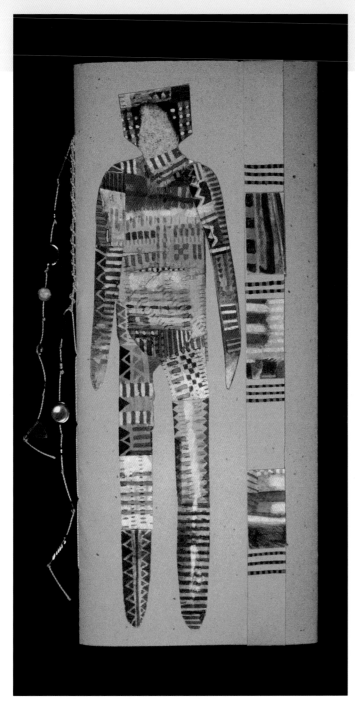

Sherrill Kahn designed this book with a watercolor collage cover and decorative stitched binding.

This journal and clamshell box by Tom Hollander was made of handmade paper with embedded fibers.

Lewis Carroll's poem *The Walrus and the Carpenter,* sung at her sixth grade graduation, inspired calligrapher Ellen Bruck to create this art journal with its unique title page and embossed cover.

Fiftieth Anniversary Album Box, by Judy Jacobs. An accordion-fold photo album forms the cover for this album box, with tiny accordion-fold books filling some of the matchbox drawers. PHOTO BY BILL WICKETT

Stream of Life, by Shireen Holman. Shireen describes this Kashmiri houseboat book as partly a memorial to her cousin, Tom Gait, whose poems are featured, and partly a thematic expression of her voyage through life, integrating the cultures of India and America. Pulp painting, letterpress printing, woodblock printing, and photo engraving.

The interior pages of *Stream of Life.*

Cookbook,
by Dorothy
Swendeman.
This fabric-covered
recipe album is
bound with plastic
turkey rings and
has pages com-
posed of plastic
bags.

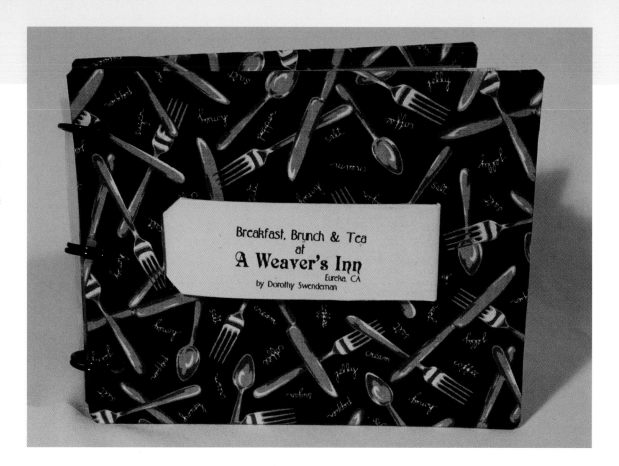

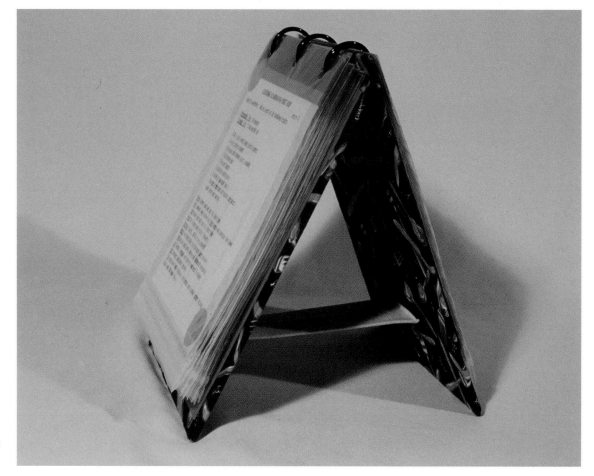

Cookbook in the
open position, with
the title strip folded
into a slot in the
back cover to create
a stand.

Unbound, by Winnie Radolan. Unbound pages of a paper-maker's journal in a sculptural clam-shell box.

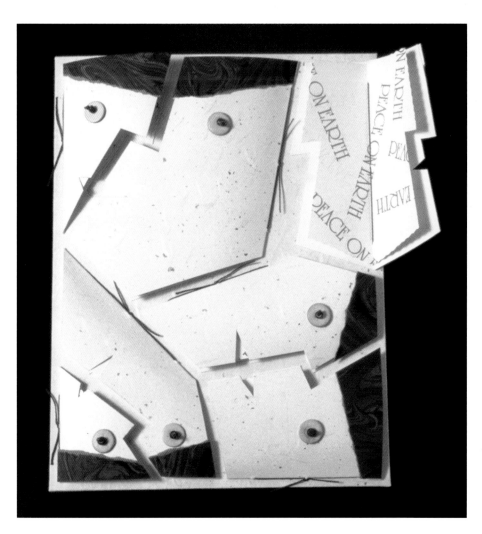

Red Heads, by Michael Jacobs. Mixed media book sculpture with pamphlet-stitched folios.

PHOTO BY BILL WICKETT

A crayon-batiked
hinged-cover scrap-
book with a varia-
tion of tortoise shell
stitching, by Gail
Crosman Moore.

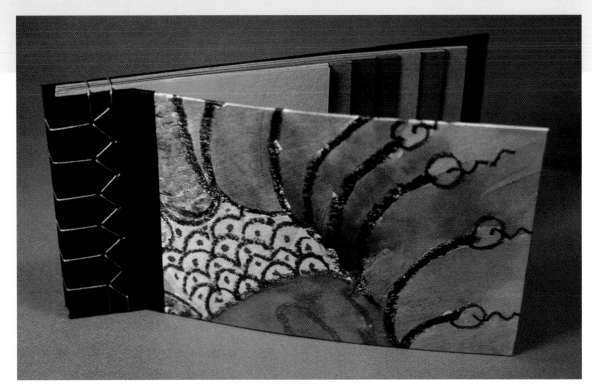

Beach Diary, by
Winnie Radolan.
Handmade paper
with stamping and
nature printing.

Bro/Repose, by Nancy Leavitt, with text by Henry De Ziel. Nancy's wire-bound accordion-fold art journal is two sided, with English on one side and Creole on the other. Gouache and glair on paste paper.

An accordion-fold photo album in suminagashi and paste papers with sculptural accents, by Diane Maurer-Mathison and Jennifer Philippoff.

FURTHER READING

Charatan, Karen. *ABC ZIG Calligraphy*. Carlstadt, New Jersey: EK Success, 1993.

Dawson, Sophie. *The Art and Craft of Papermaking*. Asheville, NC: Lark Books, 1997.

Dubay, Inga and Barbara Getty. *Italic Letters: Calligraphy & Handwriting*. Portland, Oregon: Portland State University Continuing Education Press, 1992.

Heller, Jules. *Papermaking*. New York: Watson-Guptill Publications, 1978.

Johnson, Pauline. *Creative Bookbinding*. New York: Dover, 1990.

LaPlantz, Shereen. *Cover to Cover*. Asheville, NC: Lark Books, 1995.

Maurer-Mathison, Diane with Jennifer Philippoff. *Paper Art*. New York: Watson-Guptill Publications, 1997.

Maurer-Mathison, Diane. *The Ultimate Marbling Handbook*. New York: Watson-Guptill Publications, 1999.

Smith, Keith A. and Fred Jordan. *Bookbinding for Book Artists*. New York: Keith A. Smith Books, 1998.

Webberley, Marilyn and JoAn Forsyth. *Books, Boxes and Wraps*. Kirkland, Washington: Bifocal Publishing, 1995.

SOURCE DIRECTORY

Aiko's Art Materials Import, Inc.
3347 North Clark Street
Chicago, IL 60657
Tel: (773) 404-5600
Japanese papers and art supplies

Amsterdam Art
1013 University Avenue
Berkeley, CA 94710
Tel: (510) 649-4800
Art supplies and paper

Bookmakers
6701B Lafayette Avenue
Riverdale, MD 20737
Tel: (301) 927-7787
Binding supplies

Carriage House Paper
79 Guernsey Street
Brooklyn, NY 11222
Tel: (800) 669-8781
Papermaking supplies

Colophon Book Arts Supply
3611 Ryan Street, S.E.
Lacey, WA 98503
Tel: (360) 459-2940
Binding supplies

Daniel Smith
4150 First Avenue, South
Seattle, WA 98134
Tel: (800) 426-6740
www.danielsmith.com
Art supplies and papers

Diane Maurer Hand Marbled
    Papers
P.O. Box 78
Spring Mills, PA 16875
Tel: (814) 422-8651
E-mail: DKMaurer1@aol.com
*Marbling, paste paper, and Boku
Undo dye supplies, and decorative
papers for bookbinding*

Dick Blick
P.O. Box 1267
Galesburg, IL 61402-1267
Tel: (800) 828-4548
www.dickblick.com
Art supplies and papers

Dieu Donné Papermill, Inc.
433 Broome Street
New York, NY 10013
Tel: (212) 226-0573
Papermaking supplies and paper

Dreamweaver Stencils
1335 Cindee Lane
Colton, CA 92324
Tel: (800) 565-4803
Embossing and stenciling supplies

ERA Graphics
2476 Ottawa Way
San Jose, CA 95130
Tel: (408) 364-1124
www.eragraphics.com
Large variety of unusual rubber stamps

Fascinating Folds
P.O. Box 10070
Glendale, AZ 85318
Tel: (800) 968-2418
www.fascinating-folds.com
Papers, books, and paper art supplies

La Papeterie St. Armand
3700 St. Patrick
Montreal, Quebec
H4E 1A2 Canada
Tel: (514) 931-8338
Papermaking supplies and paper

Lee S. McDonald, Inc.
P.O. Box 264
Charlestown, MA 02129
Tel: (617) 242-2505
Papermaking supplies

Light Impressions
P.O. Box 940
Rochester, NY 14603-0940
Tel: (800) 828-6216
www.lightimpressionsdirect.com
Archival supplies

Nature's Pressed
P.O. Box 212
Orem, UT 84059-0212
Tel: (800) 850-2499
www.naturespressed.com
Pressed leaves and flowers

John Neal, Bookseller
1833 Spring Garden Street
Greensboro, NC 27403
Tel: (336) 272-6139
www.johnnealbooks.com
Books and calligraphy supplies

New York Central Art Supply
62 Third Avenue
New York, NY 10003
Tel: (800) 950-6111; in New York
    state: (212) 477-0400
www.nycentralart.com
Art supplies

The Original Paper-Ya
9-1666 Johnston Street
Granville Island
Vancouver, BC
V6H 3S2 Canada
Tel: (604) 684-2531
Paper

Paper & Ink Books
P.O. Box 35
3 North Second Street
Woodsboro, MD 21798
Tel: (301) 898-7991
Books and calligraphy supplies

Paper Source, Inc.
232 W. Chicago Avenue
Chicago, IL 60610
Tel: (312) 337-0798
Large selection of papers

Pearl Paint Co. Inc.
308 Canal Street
New York, NY 10013-2572
Tel: (800) 451-PEARL
www.pearlpaint.com
Art supplies and paper

Swallow Creek Papers
P.O. Box 152
Spring Mills, PA 16875
Tel: (814) 422-8651
Decorative paper for paper crafts

TALAS
568 Broadway, Room 107
New York, NY 10012
Tel: (212) 219-0770
www.talas-nyc.com
Binding supplies

University Products, Inc.
517 Main Street
Holyoke, MA 01041-0101
Tel: (800) 628-1912
www.universityproducts.com
Archival bookmaking supplies

USArtQuest, Inc.
P.O. Box 88
Chelsea, MI 48118
Tel: (800) 200-7848
www.usartquest.com
Mica tiles and collage materials

INDEX